— night light
— water (1)
— figure
— cushion ✓
— 21 breaths

"What I am is good enough, what I am doing is good enough, What I have is good enough".

Guided Meditations on the Stages of the Path

Guided Meditations *on the* Stages of the Path

Bhikshuni Thubten Chodron

SNOW LION PUBLICATIONS

ITHACA, NEW YORK • BOULDER, COLORADO

Snow Lion Publications • P. O. Box 6483
Ithaca, NY 14851 USA • (607) 273-8519
www.snowlionpub.com

Printed in USA on acid-free recycled paper.

ISBN-10: 1-55939-281-9
ISBN-13: 978-1-55939-281-5

Designed and typeset by Gopa & Ted2, Inc.

*Library of Congress
Cataloging-in-Publication Data*

Thubten Chodron, 1950-
  Guided meditations on the stages of the path /
Bhikshuni Thubten Chodron.
    p. cm.
  Includes bibliographical references.
  ISBN-13: 978-1-55939-281-5 (alk. paper)
  ISBN-10: 1-55939-281-9 (alk. paper)
  1. Lam-rim. 2. Meditation—Buddhism.
I. Title.

BQ7645.L35T48 2007
294.3'4435—dc22

                              2007022347

Also by Thubten Chodron

Buddhism for Beginners (Snow Lion Publications)

Cultivating a Compassionate Heart: The Yoga Method of Chenrezig
(Snow Lion Publications)

Glimpse of Reality (with Dr. Alexander Berzin)

How to Free Your Mind: Tara the Liberator (Snow Lion Publications)

Open Heart, Clear Mind (Snow Lion Publications)

The Path to Happiness (Texas Buddhist Association)

Taming the Mind (Snow Lion Publications)

Working with Anger (Snow Lion Publications)

Books edited by Thubten Chodron

Blossoms of the Dharma: Living as a Buddhist Nun (North Atlantic Books, Berkeley, CA)

A Chat about Heruka, by Lama Zopa Rinpoche (Lama Yeshe Wisdom Archives)

A Chat about Yamantaka, by Lama Zopa Rinpoche (Lama Yeshe Wisdom Archives)

Choosing Simplicity: A Commentary of the Bhikshuni Pratimoksha,
by Ven. Bhikshuni Master Wu Yin (Snow Lion Publications)

Heruka Body Mandala: Sadhana and Commentary, by Ven. Lati Rinpoche

Interfaith Insights (Timeless Books, New Delhi)

Pearl of Wisdom, Books I and *II: Buddhist Prayers and Practices* (Sravasti Abbey)

*Transforming Adversity into Joy and Courage: An Explanation of the Thirty-seven
Practices of Bodhisattvas,* by Geshe Jampa Tegchok (Snow Lion Publications)

༃ — Contents ༄

THE DALAI LAMA

⌁ — Foreword — ⌁

I AM VERY HAPPY to learn that Bhikshuni Thubten Chodron has undertaken to record the analytical meditations on the Lamrim. As a bhikshuni, it is all the more encouraging to see that she has undertaken such an important task. As I often tell people, the analytical meditations on the points of the Lamrim will transform our minds and enable us to become more compassionate and wise. I encourage people to do these meditations as part of their daily practice.

February 9, 2001

INTRODUCTION

DURING HIS forty-five years of teaching throughout ancient India in the sixth century B.C.E., the Buddha had numerous discussions about spiritual views, conduct, and practice with those he encountered, be they Brahmins (who composed the religious hierarchy of his day), practitioners from other sects, or his own disciples. These teachings, or *sutras*, were passed down orally for centuries until the first century B.C.E., when they were written down. In subsequent centuries, Indian scholar-practitioners compiled and systematized the important points of the sutras by writing treatises. As Buddhism spread from India throughout Central, East, and Southeast Asia, the scholar-practitioners in these areas also wrote commentaries in order to clarify and make the principal points of the original sutras and Indian commentaries more accessible to the people of those times. The Indian sage Atisha (982-1054), in his short but profound text *Lamp of the Path*, organized the teachings into three levels of practice—initial, middle, and advanced—according to the gradual development and expansion of a person's spiritual motivation.

Later generations of Tibetan sages, in particular Je Tsongkhapa (1357-1419), systematized the teachings further, forming the *lamrim*—the stages of the path to enlightenment. His classic text, the *Lamrim Chenmo* (or *The Great Treatise on the Stages of the Path to Enlightenment*), constitutes three volumes in English translation. He wrote several other lamrim texts of various lengths as well. The teachings of the lamrim can be compared to ready-made clothes that we can easily wear; that is, the authors of the various lamrim texts systematized and explained the major points of the Buddha's teachings so that we can learn and practice them in an organized and understandable fashion.

The term "lamrim" can be translated into English in various ways, each emphasizing a slightly different aspect of its meaning. When translated as "stages of the path," we get the idea of a path with definite stages. The translation "steps on the path" gives us the feeling of movement as we take steps along the path. The translation "gradual path" connotes a steady, step-by-step progression. All of these translations and connotations are appropriate. Nevertheless, in this book, "gradual path" is generally used. Since people in modern society tend to be goal-oriented and want to hurry to finish a project, reminding us that spiritual practice is a gradual path helps us to slow down and mindfully focus on the process of transforming our mind.

These systematic teachings of the gradual path are the subject of this book and the accompanying CD. These materials are suitable for beginners, as well as intermediate and more advanced practitioners. The lamrim presents a step-by-step method to tame the mind, and each person will find meaning and insight according to his or her level of understanding. As you practice these meditations repeatedly, your comprehension and experience of them will transform and deepen even though the words used to spark your meditation sessions remain the same.

Part I of this book enables us to learn how to meditate. It discusses how to establish a daily practice, from setting up an altar to doing the two kinds of meditation—stabilizing and analytical. You will learn how to prepare your body and mind for meditation, how to practice mindfulness of breathing, and how to meditate on the gradual path.

Part II presents the meditations—meditation on the Buddha and the analytical meditations on the lamrim. The texts of various other recitations you may like to do are also included.

Part III presents supplementary material to assist you in meditating on the lamrim. This includes an overview of the gradual path to enlightenment, instructions for working with distractions, antidotes to mental afflictions, advice for newcomers, and suggestions on how to deepen your Dharma practice. An appendix with the outlines of the meditations recorded on the CD, a glossary, and a list of suggested readings are provided at the end for your convenience.

The meditations are recorded on the accompanying CD to assist you in learning the analytical, or checking, meditations on the topics of the gradual path. These recordings are guided meditations, not teachings. Ideally, they should be used in conjunction with oral teachings on the gradual path from a qualified teacher and supplemented with readings from lamrim books. However, since you may live far from your Buddhist teachers or a Dharma center, my hope is that these guided meditations will enable you to begin and continue a daily meditation practice.

ACKNOWLEDGMENTS

I pay homage to Shakyamuni Buddha, as well as to the spiritual masters of the Nalanda tradition, Lama Atisha, Je Tsongkhapa, and the lineage of spiritual mentors who preserved and transmitted the scriptures and realizations from the Buddha to the present day. In addition, I am forever indebted to my teachers for sharing the precious teachings on the gradual path with me: H. H. the Dalai Lama, Tsenzhap Serkong Rinpoche, Lama Thubten Yeshe, Zopa Rinpoche, Geshe Ngawang Dhargye, Geshe Sonam Rinchen, Khenzur Jampa Tegchok Rinpoche, Geshe Lhundrup Sopa, and many other masters who learned, practiced, actualized, and taught the meditations on the stages of the path to enlightenment.

Several people kindly assisted in the production of this CD and book. I led these guided meditations while Peter Aronson did the audio recording in 2001. Peter then edited the recording, while Kim Shetter, with assistance from Barbara McDaniel, coordinated this project. Ang Hwee Leng, Peter Aronson, and Steven Vannoy did the "proof-hearing." Lama Thubten Yeshe and Zopa Rinpoche composed the meditation on the Buddha. The chanting is the *Praises of Tara*, performed by the Tibetan Buddhist nuns of Khachoe Ghakyil Nunnery in Nepal. We appreciate receiving their permission to use it. I would also like to thank Ven. Tenzin Chogkyi who edited the manuscript of the book. All of us hope that you will find this combination of a book and CD helpful in your spiritual journey. Since some people learn better by hearing and others by reading, everyone should be able to benefit.

To learn more about Buddhism, read Dharma articles, and listen to Dharma talks online, visit www.thubtenchodron.org.

PLEASE NOTE

People who are familiar with the gradual path teachings will notice that points of the traditional lamrim outline have been altered in a few places. For example, because most Westerners were not raised Buddhist, a section with meditations that introduce the Buddhist view is included at the beginning. This will assist people who are new to Buddhism to gain some familiarity with the Buddhist concepts of mind, heart, rebirth, cyclic existence, and liberation, as well as to see how mind, thoughts, and emotions create our experience.

In the meditation on the precious human life, points mentioning the unfortunate realms have been omitted, and the points of the freedoms and fortunes have been combined. This was done to ease new practitioners into these topics. The topic of the unfortunate realms is included in the meditation on compassion as an easier way for new practitioners to understand this concept. An extensive outline for the meditation on the precious human life is included as Appendix 2 so that those who wish can do the full meditation on this topic.

The meditation on relying on a spiritual mentor is presented at the end of the gradual path, rather than the beginning, because if you are new to Buddhism, you will see the importance of cultivating a good relationship with a qualified teacher after you have an understanding of the gradual path as a whole. This follows the way in which H. H. the Dalai Lama presents the Dharma. He teaches the Buddhist worldview first, followed by the meditations to transform the mind. As a result of understanding these, people will naturally appreciate, respect, and wish to rely on a spiritual mentor in a healthy and beneficial way.

Concerning terminology, the Sanskrit term *klesha* (Pali: *kilesa*; Tibetan: *nyon mongs*) can be translated in various ways into English: mental afflictions, disturbing attitudes, and negative emotions, delusions, afflictive emotions, disturbing emotions, and so forth. In this book and the accompanying CD, many of these terms have been used interchangeably, depending on the context and the emphasis. They all refer to the collection of mental factors that disturb the mind and are the chief impediments to liberation from cyclic existence. Some of these, such as distorted views and ignorance, tend to be attitudes; others, such as anger and attachment, are more emotional in nature. All misconceive either the conventional situation or its ultimate mode of existence, thereby obscuring and disturbing the mind and motivating actions (*karma*) that disturb our lives and the lives of others.

Bhikshuni Thubten Chodron
Sravasti Abbey, Newport WA, USA
Vesak Day, May 31, 2007

PART I

Learning to Meditate

1. Introduction to Meditation

Why Meditate?

The Tibetan word for "meditate," *gom*, means "to familiarize" or "habituate." In this case, we intentionally habituate ourselves with beneficial and realistic attitudes and emotions. Thus, we familiarize ourselves with the meaning and experiences of these meditations in order to transform our minds. Similarly, the English word "practice" implies repetition and gradual development. Change does not occur suddenly but over time. We must practice continuously and meditate on the same topics repeatedly to gain familiarity with them and to shift our perspective.

The Buddha's teachings describe meditation as the last of the trilogy of hearing (which includes studying and reading), thinking, and meditating. We begin by studying the Buddha's teachings so that we will understand the role of meditation and the correct way to meditate. Then we think about these teachings, discuss them with others, and ask questions in order to assure that we correctly understand them. Finally, we integrate them with our mind and heart through meditating on them.

Some people would like to begin with meditation, and while their motivation may be sincere, they often encounter difficulties. If we do not first learn the proper way to meditate, we may try to do so but our efforts will not be successful. Furthermore, we may meditate incorrectly, which would obscure our mind even further. However, if we begin by studying the Dharma (the Buddha's teachings), over the long term our practice will be more stable. We will gain an overall view of our present situation and have a sense of the direction in which we want to progress spiritually. We will also have the correct motivation for meditation, which is essential for accomplishing our sincere spiritual goals. For all these reasons, the great sages advise that we undertake all three activities—studying, thinking, and meditating.

Two Types of Meditation

There are two principal types of meditation: stabilizing meditation and checking (analytical) meditation. The former is done primarily to develop single-pointed concentration (*samadhi*) and serenity (*shamatha*) and the latter is done principally to cultivate understanding and special insight (*vipashyana*). To attain liberation and enlightenment, mastery of both forms of meditation is necessary. Some people think that concentration alone is sufficient to gain liberation. While they may gain single-pointed concentration by doing stabilizing meditation, their concentration will only suppress the gross afflictions temporarily. They will appear again once the state of concentration ends. However, direct realization of the ultimate nature of reality—the emptiness of inherent existence—eradicates the afflictions and their seeds from our mental continuum in such a way that they no longer exist. Such a profound realization depends on developing the union of serenity and special insight.

To gain a correct realization of emptiness, we must first have a correct conceptual understanding of it. While direct nonconceptual realization is our ultimate goal, we cannot actualize it immediately. Just saying "I will meditate to realize emptiness" over and over does not help us realize it. Similarly meditating on our made-up assumption of what emptiness means does not lead to insight. We may mistakenly think that the "empty" in "all phenomena are empty" has the same meaning as in "the refrigerator is empty."

For these reasons, we must first hear teachings about emptiness and then think deeply about them so that we gain an accurate conceptual understanding. Next we meditate on this understanding in order to gain a conceptual realization of emptiness. This is followed by actualizing the union of serenity and special insight, which union directly and nonconceptually realizes emptiness. This realization of the ultimate nature is what will gradually cleanse our mindstream of all defilements. Here we see that thinking about emptiness is necessary, even though later on the path our meditation will go beyond thoughts and concepts.

Analytical meditation trains our mind to use reasoning in order to reduce mental afflictions. Subtler levels of analytical meditation go beyond thought and scrutinize the meditation object so that we can thoroughly understand and penetrate it. Using analysis or examination when meditating does not mean intellectually thinking about a topic. We don't dryly recite, "The first point is ABC. The second point is XYZ." Nor are we stuck in our head conceptualizing about abstract phenomena. Rather, analysis means checking, investigating, and seeing for ourselves what something is and how it relates to our lives. Initially this may involve thinking, but this is not discursive, intellectual thinking. In more advanced stages of analytical meditation, wisdom scrutinizes how things exist without employing thought.

A proper motivation for meditation is also essential because the results of our endeavors depend upon the motivation with which we do them. If we take the time necessary to build a strong and stable foundation, the rest of our Dharma practice will progress well. If we don't, it is similar to someone trying to construct an elaborate roof on a weak foundation.

Since gaining a direct, nonconceptual realization of emptiness takes time, we must first learn antidotes that are easier to apply and use them to temporarily subdue our afflictions. For example, while the wisdom realizing the emptiness of inherent existence will eradicate anger from its root so that it can never arise in our minds again, meditation on patience and love will reduce it in the interim. Thus we practice patience and love and employ them to subdue our anger now, while also cultivating the wisdom realizing emptiness, which will eventually eliminate it from the root.

Analytical meditation on the gradual path to enlightenment has many benefits: it leads to a complete understanding of the path to enlightenment, helps us to generate a proper motivation for Dharma practice, and develops our meditative abilities.

In addition, it is useful for cultivating the antidotes that temporarily counteract the afflictions.

There is another way of speaking about the two types of meditation. In this case, they are differentiated into 1) meditation that perceives the object and 2) meditation in which our mind is transformed into a specific affective state. An example of the former is meditating on impermanence and emptiness. These are subtle objects that we must use analytical meditation to perceive. An example of the latter is meditation on the four immeasurables (*brahmaviharas*)—love, compassion, joy, and equanimity. Here we are not trying to perceive a subtle object, but are practicing to transform our minds into those mental states. For example, everyone admires the quality of love, but we cannot just say, "I should love everyone," and expect our deepest feelings to change. First, we must free our minds from the gross obstacles of attachment to friends, hostility to people who threaten or harm us, and apathy towards strangers. On this basis, we then train our mind to recognize the kindness of others, which arouses in us a natural wish to reciprocate and share our kindness with them. After this we meditate on love and cultivate a genuine wish for all sentient beings to have happiness and its causes. Initially that feeling will arise in us but will not be stable. Anger may still flash into our mind making our good feelings towards others disappear. We need to cultivate love continuously and do so with a focused mind. The greater our concentration, the more stable and penetrative the experience will be.

How to Use These Guided Meditations

Find a quiet place in your home and if you wish, set up an altar with a Buddha image and offerings as described in the chapter "Preparing for Meditation." Sit comfortably on a cushion or a chair with your hands in your lap, palms up, the right on the left with your thumbs touching. Keep your head level and lower your eyes. Begin each meditation session with:

1. the meditation on the Buddha along with recitations to prepare your mind and set your motivation. You can do these recitations quickly (track 4 on the CD),

or take more time with the visualizations and contemplations that accompany them (track 2).

2. a body scan to establish a firm but relaxed meditation posture
3. several minutes of breathing meditation to free the mind from distractions. (Track 3 will guide you through the body scan and breathing meditation.)

These three points will be explained in more depth in future chapters. The chapter "Preparing for Meditation" contains instructions on topics such as setting up an altar, meditation posture, and preparing your body and mind for meditation. "Mindfulness of Breathing" explains one way to do the breathing meditation. The text for the meditation on the Buddha is in a chapter with that title, and an outline of this practice is in "Establishing a Daily Practice."

Please note: some people find it more effective to establish their motivation, do the body scan and mindfulness of breathing, and then do the meditation on the Buddha and the recitations, followed by checking meditation on a lamrim topic. Either order is fine.

Having prepared your mind in this way, do one of the meditations on the gradual path to enlightenment found in subsequent tracks. Meditating while listening to the guided meditation is an excellent way to become familiar with and contemplate each topic. If you would like to meditate longer on a particular point, press the pause button and meditate on that point for as long as you wish before continuing. (However, don't fast-forward if you're feeling impatient!)

The points of each meditation are found in the chapter "Lamrim Meditation Outlines." If you wish to guide yourself through the topic, read the first point on the meditation outline, contemplate it, read the next point, contemplate it, and so forth. If you do this, you may want to precede your meditation session by reading a section from a book on the topic you will be contemplating and jotting down a few notes in order to incorporate those points into your meditation session.

Regardless of whether you listen to the recorded meditation or read the meditation outline, first do checking meditation on that particular lamrim topic. Here, investigate that topic taught by the Buddha in order to understand it deeply. Think about the topic applying reasoning. In addition, relate the topic to your personal experience. When you have a deep feeling or strong experience of the meaning of that meditation, focus on just that experience with stabilizing meditation, concentrating on it single-pointedly so that it becomes part of you. In this way, do both analytical meditation by reflecting on the points in the outline and stabilizing meditation by remaining one-pointedly on the conclusion in one meditation session.

At the conclusion of the meditation session dedicate the positive potential by reciting the dedication verses (track 5) or by expressing a dedication in your own words. After meditating you may want to sit quietly and absorb what you reflected on for a few minutes before engaging in your daily activities.

For an expanded explanation of the practice of checking meditation and of its role in our overall practice, see *Transforming Adversity into Joy and Courage* by Geshe Jampa Tegchok, pages 52–53.

Please remember that these meditations are not philosophical exercises, but are intended to touch us profoundly and effect deep change within us when we do them repeatedly over a period of time. Apply the points in each meditation to help you understand your mind, emotions, and reactions. Meditation is a quiet time for more concentrated reflection, but its purpose is to affect our thoughts, feelings, words, and actions. Thus, integrate what you learn in meditation with your daily life activities and interactions with others. Similarly, bring your life into your practice by investigating and using your daily experiences as examples when you do the checking meditations.

Cycle through the entire lamrim outline, going through the checking meditations one by one, in order, focusing on one topic each day. A particular meditation might touch you in a deep way, and you may want to stay with that one for a few days. That is fine. When you have completed the cycle of all the checking meditations, begin again.

You will notice that each time you cycle through this series of meditations you will see new connections among them. Also, each time you do a particular meditation your experience will be different. Sometimes you will go slower than other times, or perhaps a different point in the outline will speak to your heart. Sometimes you will have strong feelings or come to a clear conclusion at the end of a meditation. Other times you may not. This is normal. Some days you may have a problem in your life that you know doing a specific meditation could help you resolve. Go ahead and do that, even if it is out of sequence. Practicing Dharma means transforming your mind, so if a particular negative emotion is arising in your mind that day, do the meditation that will help you to release it.

As you cycle through the meditations, approach each one freshly. Do not try to re-create a previous experience. Avoid labeling a meditation session "good" or "bad" depending on your feelings just afterwards. We cannot immediately see the effects of practice. It affects us in subtle ways and its results are cumulative over time. As His Holiness the Dalai Lama recommends, do not expect big changes in a short time. Instead, observe the transformation that has occurred in you after one year, five years, or ten years. Simply be content to create the causes for goodness.

This book and CD are only a beginning. Each topic is more vast than the summarized points recorded here. Please continue to study by attending oral teachings by qualified spiritual masters and by reading books on the topics of the stages of the path to enlightenment. As you do, bring what you learn into your meditations and expand on the outlines presented here. It is wise to check your meditation experiences with a teacher. If you have difficulties, seek advice. If you have insights, seek further guidance. However, in either case, do not get attached to whatever you experience. Simply learn from it and dedicate it for the benefit of all beings.

2. Establishing a Daily Practice

Introduction

How to start a daily practice is a topic of concern for many people who attend classes at a Dharma center and for people who read about Buddhism but lack access to a Dharma teacher or center in their area. They like what they learn and want to know how to put it into practice, but they wonder, "What do I do now?"

Within Tibetan Buddhism there are many different kinds of practices. In addition, our teachers continuously give instructions on new ones. You may become confused, thinking, "What am I supposed to do? This is overwhelming. Should I do prostrations, lamrim meditation, serenity meditation, animal liberation, water bowls, mandala offerings, Chenrezig meditation, Mahamudra, Dzogchen, or what?"

Different Buddhist teachers will give different answers to this question. Here I will describe the responses of my teachers, most of whom are spiritual descendants of Je Tsongkhapa. This is advice they gave to those of us who were the first generation of non-Tibetan practitioners of Tibetan Buddhism. His Holiness the Dalai Lama reaffirms this method in his public teachings, and speaking personally, I have found it very helpful.

First of all, build your daily practice in a gradual way. When you begin, your body isn't used to sitting for long periods. You may have a lot of enthusiasm for Buddhist practice and think, "I'm going to be a great yogi and sit for two hours in the morning and two hours in the evening in single-pointed meditation." Most of us quickly realize that we can't do this, unless we are one of the very few people who has strong, excellent karmic latencies from previous lives. For most of us, it is better to start out with short meditation sessions of a comfortable duration, so that at the end of a meditation session we don't feel exhausted. Instead we feel inspired and are eager to return to our meditation cushion later on. It is better to have several shorter sessions, rather than one long session in which we push ourselves and then feel like it has all become too much.

Practicing every day is important. We each have a daily routine—our own daily rituals. If we include morning meditation in our routine, then meditating every morning becomes very easy. It becomes natural: we wake up, set our motivation, brush our teeth, make offerings to the Buddha, make a cup of tea, and meditate. Then we have breakfast and begin the day's activities. In this way, our practice will progress gradually and naturally, without pushing. Each day we build on what we did the previous day, or at least maintain the same energy. On the other hand, if we practice sporadically—let's say meditating five hours one day and then not at all for the rest of the week—we lose our momentum and have to build it up again. Meditation is like any skill. It requires consistent practice. For example, when someone wants to learn to play a musical instrument, she must practice every day. Playing only once a week doesn't bring continual progress. Learning to meditate works in the same way.

You might think, "I don't have time to meditate every day." However, we have time to eat every day, to talk to our friends, to go here and there. It's actually a matter of priorities. We nourish and rest our body daily because our physical health is important. Our spiritual and mental health is just as important, so let's make sure to nourish our mind and heart on a daily basis as well. Doing so not only benefits our mind, but also contributes to our physical health, because less stress in the mind means less stress in the body. Daily practice also benefits those close to you. When you are calmer, your relationships with the people you live with and with friends and colleagues improve.

Waking Up in the Morning

The way we wake up in the morning is very important as it influences our moods and feelings during the rest of the day. These, in turn, affect our motivations, and our motivations are the chief factor in the kind of karma we create during the day. Our mind is especially subtle in the morning, so whatever we encounter or think has a strong effect. If we wake up to music, that melody may float through our mind when we later sit down to meditate. If we wake up to the radio news, "fifteen people killed in Iraq" or "The CEO of Enron convicted" or "Internet pornography ring discovered," we will likely go through the day feeling despair about the world's situation. Or we may tune it out and feel apathetic about others. Neither of these attitudes is conducive for spiritual progress. Therefore, it's important to wake up as peacefully as possible and immediately direct our minds in a constructive way. By practicing this repeatedly now, when we "wake up" to our next life, we will be much more likely to generate a positive motivation at that time as well.

Right away, when you wake up, think, "How wonderful! I still have a precious human life with the opportunity to practice the Dharma. I take refuge in my spiritual mentors and in the Three Jewels—the Buddhas, Dharma, and Sangha." Then contemplate, "The most important thing I have to do today is to avoid harming others as much as possible. Another important thing is to help others as much as I am able, in any way, whether large or small. The third important element is to hold the *bodhicitta*—the altruistic intention aspiring to attain full enlightenment in order to be able to benefit all sentient beings most effectively—foremost in my heart and to do all actions with this as my long-term motivation."

At first this motivation may seem strange because according to our usual way of thinking the most important thing to do today is to meet a certain client, to pick the kids up from school, or to clean out the garage. But if you think about it, we do these activities and then forget about them. In a year we won't even remember having done them. In addition, we are not usually thinking of everyone's long-term benefit when we engage in these daily activities; rather, we are thinking of what will make our life easier and how we will profit.

Our motivation for doing any of the activities we engage in is critical. Thus, remembering not to harm others, to help them, and to hold the bodhicitta dear are most important in any activity we do during the day. In this way, all our activities become beneficial for both ourselves and others, and lead to enlightenment.

By setting our motivation strongly in the morning when our mind is fresh and clear, we are much more likely to remember it during the day and act with that intention. In addition, picking something that happens frequently during the day to act as a kind of "mindfulness bell" or trigger to bring us back to our positive motivation is very helpful. For example, every time you stop at a stop light, come back to your breath and remember bodhicitta. Every time the phone rings, pause and remember bodhicitta before you answer it. One person told me that her trigger was her child calling, "Mommyyyyyy!" She would pause, breathe, remember her good intention, and then attend to her child. Doing this helped her not only spiritually but also in the moment, for she could care for her child in a calm manner.

GETTING TO THE MEDITATION CUSHION

Establish your motivation as soon as you wake up, before you get out of bed. If you tend to forget, put a post-it in a place where you will see it, for example on your nightstand or on the bathroom mirror. Then wash your face or shower, transforming that action by thinking that you are cleansing ignorance, anger, and attachment from your mind and the minds of all sentient beings as you bathe. If you wish, have a cup of tea and then sit down to meditate. Don't read the paper, turn on the TV, or start your daily chores. If you'd like, read from a Dharma book while you drink your tea, but don't linger at the kitchen table. Go to the place where you meditate.

Meditate every day, preferably at the same time. The morning is best because the mind is fresher and not full of thoughts and feelings about the day's activities. Some people prefer to meditate in the evening, and that is fine, although it can be more challenging to get to the meditation cushion after a busy day. If you can meditate at both times, it's even better. However, don't think, "I'll just take care of this little thing and then go to meditate," because before you know it, you've gotten involved in a lot of activities. By doing your practice first thing in the morning, you are setting the stage for what will happen the rest of the day by cultivating your good intentions. In general, having a regular schedule of when you wake up, meditate, eat, and go to sleep is helpful.

Sometimes we get to the cushion and thoughts come, "I should return this phone call," "the children need me," "I found the solution to the problem we were dealing with at work yesterday." These are all ego's tricks to distract us from what is important. When these thoughts arise, stop and ask yourself, "Is there anything that desperately needs to be done in the next half an hour, such that somebody is going to be drastically harmed if I don't do it?" If the answer is "No," then do your practice and don't worry about anything. This way of checking in with ourselves enables us to confirm that we have the time to meditate.

Just as nourishing our body every day is important and we take time to eat, nourishing ourselves spiritually is also essential. Meditation is time to become friends with ourselves. It is not selfish to each day make a time to be quiet, be in the present moment, and nourish our good qualities. By cultivating our own good qualities and letting ourselves be content, we are able to give more to others during the rest of the day.

Consistency in your meditation practice is important, and on the days when you feel lazy or rushed, some self-discipline may be necessary. If you have difficulty finding time for Dharma practice, write in your daily calendar that you have an appointment with the Buddha at a certain time. If you want to meditate for fifteen, thirty, or sixty minutes each morning, schedule it in your calendar. Later, if someone calls and wants you to do something else at that time, you can truthfully say, "I'm sorry, I have an appointment that I can't break." If you have to excuse yourself from an activity in order to go to bed a little earlier so that you are well rested for your appointment with the Enlightened One in the morning, do that. We don't stand up dates with our friends just because we're tired or have other things to do, so we should certainly keep our appointments with the Buddha.

Make your sessions moderate in length, so that you feel refreshed at the end.

Initially, this may be only ten or fifteen minutes. Gradually extend your sessions as your body and mind become used to meditating.

Sometimes parents say, "I can't take time out to meditate because the children require attention." When you are flustered and rushed, the quality of attention you give to your children is lacking. Parents often complain that their children don't know how to sit still and be quiet. However, if they've only seen their parents rush from one activity to the next and have never seen them sit quietly and contentedly, the children have no example to follow. Sometimes the greatest gift you can give to your child is to let him or her see you being peaceful and content.

If you need to get up a little earlier so that you can meditate before the children wake up, it is well worth it. Some parents alternate meditating so one can care for a baby. Other times, they bring a young child into the room with them. The child may enjoy sitting quietly or coloring peacefully while the parents meditate. Children often love the sound of chanting. They feel loved when they sit in their parent's lap and listen to the parent chant verses or mantras. Please don't underestimate your child's ability to understand the value of being peaceful. Give your child the opportunity to enjoy quiet, to slow down, to be content with the present moment. However, don't expect a young child to stay quietly for a long meditation session.

Once in the room where you meditate, there are various steps that help us prepare for meditation, such as setting up an altar, making offerings, sitting in proper meditation posture, and so on. The chapter entitled "Preparing for Meditation" explains these preliminary practices in more detail.

EVENING MEDITATION

In the evening, when you come home, do another meditation session if possible. Don't wait until right before you go to sleep because you may be too tired to meditate then. Instead, meditate in the late afternoon or early evening. In this session, review the day's events, being particularly aware of what you thought, felt, said, and did. In the morning you set your motivation not to harm, to benefit others as much as possible, and to hold the bodhicitta aspiration. In the evening, check up and evaluate how you did. Ask yourself, "How did I do in terms of living the compassionate motivation I cultivated this morning? How well was I able to live my Dharma values? Where are areas for improvement?"

Doing this, you may discover that you got irritated at somebody at work. However, unlike before, you did not speak rudely to him. There are two things here: the anger in the mind and the controlled speech. First, rejoice that you restrained yourself from harmful speech. This was an improvement compared to how you would have reacted in the past. You did not hurt the other person by denigrating him, nor did you plant negative karmic seeds in your own mind from harsh speech. Rejoicing in your improved behavior and virtuous actions is important. In this way you encourage yourself to continue being aware of your speech and to refrain from harming others or yourself by speaking harsh words.

Then reflect on the anger that was in your mind. Some of it may still be there, hours later. Going to sleep with such a state of mind may lead to restless sleep and waking up grouchy. To release any remaining irritation or anger, apply a Dharma antidote. Some of the counterforces to anger are included in the chapter "Antidotes to the Mental Afflictions." Others may be found in Chapter Six of Shantideva's *Guide to the Bodhisattva's Way of Life* or in books such as *Healing Anger* and *Working with Anger*. By doing these meditations in the evening, your mind will become calm and you will be able to sleep peacefully and wake up refreshed, with enthusiasm to generate a wholesome motivation.

Or, let's say you were not careful when you got irritated at your colleague and spoke to him in a sarcastic manner. Regardless of whether or not he made a mistake, your harmful intention and demeaning speech are not conducive to your own well-being now or in the future. Since negative karmic seeds from that action remain on your mindstream, you will want to do some purification practice to eliminate them and to prevent yourself from developing a habit of ill will and sarcastic speech. The Vajrasattva meditation and prostrations to the thirty-five Buddhas are excellent in this regard. These may be found in the *Pearl of Wisdom* prayer books or other practice manuals.

It is also helpful to meditate on emptiness in the evening, contemplating especially the lack of inherent existence of both your destructive karma and your positive potential. Doing an extended dedication of positive potential in the evening is also beneficial. Rejoicing at and dedicating your own and others' goodness uplifts your mind, encourages you to continue practicing the next day, and increases your positive potential. Please see the chapter "Additional Dedication Verses" for more extended dedications.

To summarize this way to begin a regular daily meditation practice: In the morning set your motivation, prepare your body and mind for meditation, practice mindfulness of breathing, do the meditation on the Buddha and an analytical meditation on the gradual path. In the evening review the day, purify, rejoice, and dedicate. As you become more familiar with the Dharma, you may want to revise this slightly or add other practices. For example, you may prefer to meditate on Chenrezig, Tara, or Manjushri in the morning in place of the meditation on the Buddha. Or, you may want to extend the time for meditation on the gradual path or do more intense meditation on bodhicitta or on the empty nature of phenomena.

3. Preparing for Meditation

THE BETTER PREPARED we are for an activity, the better that activity goes. For example, if we have a kitchen that is easy to navigate and contains all the ingredients we need, cooking a tasty meal will not be difficult. Similarly, when we prepare properly for a meditation session, the time spent meditating is more enjoyable and fruitful. The texts on the gradual path to enlightenment list six preparatory practices to do preceding meditation on the lamrim:

1. Find a quiet place to meditate, clean the area, and arrange an altar.
2. Make offerings.
3. Prepare your body and mind by sitting in a comfortable position, examining your mind for distractions, and cultivating a beneficial motivation.
4. Visualize the field of positive potential.
5. Purify negativities and create positive potential through the seven-limb prayer and offering the mandala.
6. Request the lineage of spiritual mentors for inspiration.

In addition, know what practice you are going to do and be familiar with the instructions or the outline on how to do it. Let's learn about each of these.

SETTING UP A PLACE TO MEDITATE, CLEANING THE AREA, AND ARRANGING AN ALTAR

Choose a quiet place to meditate. Meditating in the same room with the TV, computer, a telephone, or your children's playthings will create distraction. If you can set aside a "quiet room" where anyone in the family can go when he or she wants to be centered and peaceful, that is good. If not, select an uncluttered part of a room where you can set up an altar and place your meditation cushion.

Keep that area clean and tidy so that the environment reflects the state of mind you want to cultivate. You may wish to sweep or dust it each day before you sit to meditate. Don't bring work items or food into that area.

Setting up an altar or shrine helps us get in touch with our spiritual side. Make the shrine higher than your meditation cushion, so that what you place on top of the altar is at eye level or higher. In the center place a statue or picture of Shakyamuni Buddha. You may want to place photos of one or more of your spiritual mentors above that. On the Buddha's right, that is, on the left side of the altar as you look at it, place a Dharma text, preferably one of the Perfection of Wisdom sutras, such as the *Heart Sutra*. On the Buddha's left (on the right as you look at the altar), place a stupa, a bell, or a picture of either of them. In this way, your altar contains representations of the enlightened body, speech, and mind: the Buddha image symbolizes the enlightened body, the text represents the enlightened speech, and the stupa or bell symbolizes the enlightened mind. If you admire particular deities such as Chenrezig (Avalokiteshvara) or Tara, place their pictures on the altar or on the wall behind the shrine.

Having an altar helps us not only when we meditate but also at other times. When we look at it before we meditate, we remember the Buddha's wonderful qualities and are inspired to practice in order to become like the Buddha and our spiritual mentors. When we happen to glance at it during the day, our attention comes home to our spiritual motivation. In addition, when we see the Buddha sitting peacefully, we remember that it's possible for us to let go of stress. When we see the calm, smiling faces of our spiritual mentors, we can smile back at them, getting in touch with our own kindness and joy.

You may wonder if having an altar really helps. What we see influences us. Imagine that instead of the peaceful figure of the Buddha you were to see a newspaper clipping with a mangled body or a magazine photo of a movie star standing in a sexy pose frequently during the day. How would that affect your mind?

Some people would like to put photos of people they love on the altar. It's more appropriate to place these on a different table. Although we care about them, seeing their picture when we're meditating may cause us to think about them, which would distract us from our meditation.

MAKING OFFERINGS

Making offerings to the Three Jewels is a wonderful daily practice. Recalling enlightened qualities and cultivating a generous attitude and delight in giving is a wonderful way to start the day. The joy we feel when our heart is open and we want to share with others is a result of our practice of generosity. Due to the change in our minds that occurs when we offer, we create positive potential (or good karma), which becomes the cause to have happiness in the future. Specifically, being generous now creates the cause to have the requisites for living—food, clothing, shelter, and medicine—as well as wealth in future lives.

Making offerings is a practice for accumulating positive potential and for purifying clinging and miserliness. Enlightened beings, such as the Buddha, do not need our offerings, respect, or prostrations. Rather, we do these practices because of the transformative effect they have on our own mind.

We can offer anything we consider beautiful on the altar. Traditionally, people offer flowers, incense, lights, and food. In the Tibetan tradition, there is the custom of offering seven bowls of water. To make the water bowl offering, begin by wiping each bowl with a clean cloth, imagining you are cleaning the defilements from the minds of sentient beings as you do so. After cleaning the bowls, place them upside down on the altar; just as we wouldn't invite a guest to our home and offer them nothing, we don't place empty bowls upright on the altar. Next, fill the first bowl with some water. Then pour most of the water into the second bowl but leave a little in the bottom of the first bowl. Place the first bowl on the altar. Then pour most of the water from the second bowl into the third, leaving a little water in the bottom of the second bowl, and place the second bowl to the right of the first one, near it, but not touching it—the distance of about a rice grain. Proceed to fill the rest of the bowls in this way, leaving a little water in each bowl as you fill the next one in sequence. Then go back to the first bowl and fill it nearly to the top, but not to overflowing—about a rice grain's distance from the top. Fill the other bowls in the same way. Recite *om ah hum*, the mantra representing the Buddha's body, speech, and mind, to consecrate the offerings. You may also want to recite the long offering mantra:

om namo bhagavate bendzay sarwaparma dana tathagataya arhate
samyaksam buddhaya tayata om bendzay bendzay maha bendzay maha
taydza bendzay maha bidya bendzay maha bodhicitta bendzay maha
bodhi mendo pasam kramana bendzay sarwa karma awarana bisho dana
bendzay soha

While filling the bowls, imagine that you are offering huge jeweled bowls filled with blissful wisdom nectar to all the Buddhas and bodhisattvas. Your offerings are luminous and fill the entire sky. The holy beings receive them and experience great bliss, as do you.

Offer water that has eight qualities, each one representing a quality that you will develop in the future as a result of offering the water with a good motivation now:

1. Your ethics will be pure because the water you offer is cool.
2. Because the water is delicious, you will come to enjoy delicious food.
3. The lightness of the water indicates that your mind and body will become fit.
4. The water's softness results in a gentle mindstream.
5. A clear mind results from the water's clearness.
6. Its being free from a bad smell will purify your karmic obscurations.
7. Because the water does not hurt the stomach, your body will be free of illness.
8. Its being easy on the throat indicates you will come to have pleasant speech.

You may want to offer bowls with the eight offerings that hosts made to their guests in ancient India. In this case, the bowls are arranged from left to right as you look at the altar, with the following offerings: water for drinking, water for washing the feet, flowers, incense, light, perfume, food, and music.

Many of these offerings have symbolic meanings. Flowers represent the qualities of the Buddhas and bodhisattvas; incense signifies the fragrance of pure ethics. Light symbolizes wisdom, and perfume represents faith and confidence in the holy beings. Offering food represents the nourishment of meditative concentration, and music reminds us of impermanence and the empty nature of all phenomena.

Instead of offering water bowls or the eight offerings, you may choose simply to place a plate with fruit or other delicious food on the altar. When you do so, offer fresh food, not leftovers. Imagine that the entire sky is filled with delicious food that satisfies the hunger and thirst of sentient beings as well as brings bliss to the Buddhas and bodhisattvas. Recite *om ah hum* or the long offering mantra as above.

You may offer electric lights; candles are not necessary. Be sensitive to others in the environment if you burn incense because some people may have allergic reactions. In this case, place the incense in a container outside to burn.

As you offer, you may also meditate on emptiness, the ultimate nature of all persons and phenomena, by contemplating:

1. You, as the one making the offering, are empty of true existence.
2. The act of offering is empty of true existence.
3. The offerings themselves are empty of true existence.
4. The Buddhas and bodhisattvas to whom you offer are empty of true existence.
5. The positive potential created by offering is empty of true existence.

Remove the seven water bowls in the evening. To empty them, start with the bowl on the right and pour it into a container. Then empty the next bowl on the right and so on until they are all emptied and placed upside down. If the bowls can air dry without staining, simply place them upside down on the shrine. Otherwise, dry them with a clean cloth, imagining that you are eliminating sentient beings' sufferings and their causes. The water can be used to water plants, or it can be poured outside in a clean area, where people do not walk.

Food may remain on the altar for a day or two if it will not spoil. Then, asking the Buddha's permission, remove the food. You may give it to friends or eat it yourself. If you eat it, please eat mindfully, thinking that the food was given to you by the Buddha. Avoid removing a delicious food offering just at the time when you happen to want to eat it.

Flowers may remain on the altar until they begin to wilt, then remove them and if possible, put them outdoors in a place where no one will step over them. Electric lights may be left on all day and night, or they may be turned off at night if it disturbs the sleep of someone nearby. If you offer the light of a candle, snuff it out at the end of your session; try to do this by some means other than blowing on it. I once lived at a Dharma center where a wing had been gutted by fire due to an altar candle having tipped over when no one was present. You can light the same candle the next day, again offering its light.

PREPARING YOUR BODY AND MIND

Set up a meditation cushion in front of the altar. While some people prefer to sit flat on the cushion, your legs are less likely to fall asleep if your buttocks are raised. Before sitting down, bow three times to show your respect for the Three Jewels—the Buddhas, Dharma, and Sangha. You may chant the mantra *om namo manjushriye namo sushriye namo uttama shriye soha* while bowing.

Sit in the seven-point meditation position, which enables the energies in the body to flow easily. This, in turn, facilitates concentration. The seven points are:

1. The optimal position is the vajra position: the right foot on the left thigh and the left foot on the right thigh. Alternatively, you can sit in the half-vajra, with the left foot on the right thigh and the right leg flat on the cushion. Or you could sit as Tara does, with both legs flat on the cushion, the left one closer to the body. Other people prefer to sit with the legs crossed in a normal way. If it helps,

you may put a small cushion under each knee. If these postures are uncomfortable, you may sit in a straight-back chair and place your feet flat on the floor.

2. The back is straight.
3. Shoulders are level.
4. The right hand is on the left, with your thumbs touching to form a triangle. Place your hands on your lap against your body.
5. The head is slightly inclined but not drooping.
6. The mouth is closed, and the tongue is placed against the upper palate.
7. The eyes are slightly open, gazing downward toward the tip of your nose or the floor, but do not focus them on anything.

Now feel your body sitting on the cushion or chair. Be "inside your body," that is, experience your body. Don't look at your body as if you were outside of it, looking at it. Be in the room, on the cushion, in the present moment.

Scan your body to release tension. One way to do this is to begin with the feet and legs, then move to the belly and lower abdomen, then the chest, back, arms, and shoulders, and finally the neck, jaw, and face. As you observe the sensations in each place, check for tension. For example, some people store their tension in their belly, others in their shoulders, still others clench their jaw. Release tension in each spot as you discover it. Then, be aware of sitting in a firm, yet relaxed, position.

CULTIVATING A PROPER MOTIVATION

To calm your mind and free it from distracting thoughts, observe your breath for a few minutes. Then cultivate a good motivation. Putting your heart into your practice is very important. For that reason it is good to begin any activity, especially a meditation session, by cultivating your motivation.

You may begin by asking yourself, "Why am I meditating?" Sit and observe the reasons that spring up in your mind. They may be, "I want to be more relaxed," or "I'm angry and want to be calm," or "My friend or teacher said meditating will help me so I want to try it." Whatever your motivation is, don't judge it. Just observe.

Sometimes our initial motivation seeks the immediate benefits we hope to receive from the meditation session. This is a limited motivation, and so it is beneficial to expand it because our motivation is the primary factor determining the result of an action. A small motivation brings a limited result. Progressively more vast, inclusive, and long-term motivations are causes for progressively more excellent results. For example, if our motivation for an activity is our own happiness now, we may or may not succeed in getting what we want. If our motivation is to prepare to die peacefully and have a good rebirth, our action will create the cause for that. If our motivation is to liberate ourselves from cyclic existence, our action will be part of the causes that bring that result. If our motivation is to attain full enlightenment in order to have full compassion, wisdom, and skillful means to benefit all sentient beings, that will be the long-term outcome of our action.

Sometimes when we observe our meditation at the beginning of a session, we discover that we're thinking, "Why am I sitting here meditating? What does that accomplish? I should be doing something useful like making money!" Such doubt is another way the self-centered attitude tries to distract us from doing what is beneficial. To counteract this, remember that we have the Buddha potential as well as a precious human life with all the conducive circumstances to make our life highly meaningful. This gives us more energy and our horizon expands: "I'm going to meditate in order to understand and apply the Dharma to my mind, thus purifying and transforming my mind for the benefit of each and every living being so that in the long-term all of us will become fully enlightened Buddhas."

You can build your motivation in a number of ways by briefly reflecting on various aspects of the Dharma. No matter whether you begin by reflecting on your precious human life, impermanence, the kindness of others, or other topics, make your conclusion, "Therefore, I want to attain the full enlightenment of a Buddha in order to benefit all sentient beings most effectively." Spend as long as you wish cultivating your motivation. Habituating ourselves with this long-term motivation gives us the ability to sustain our practice over time. It also makes our mind stronger and more courageous. Joy begins to grow because we know that we're going in a good direction—we are headed towards enlightenment no matter how long it takes to get there.

Then when we go through a rough period when our mind is very unruly, our body is ill, or we face other problems, we won't despair. Instead, we will know in our hearts, "I'm glad to see these mental afflictions because now I can clean them up" or "Problems are bearable. They won't overwhelm me. I can transform them into the path to actualize the noblest aspiration, bodhicitta."

Reading an inspiring passage from the *Dhammapada* or another Dharma book will invigorate your motivation. Or, you may reflect on the advantages of meditation and the disadvantages of letting our mind run untamed. Remembering the example of your spiritual mentor's compassion and wisdom will inspire you to want to develop those qualities within yourself. Alternatively, think in the following way:

At the moment I have a precious human life with all the conditions conducive for spiritual practice. I am healthy and have met the Dharma, a teacher who instructs me, and other practitioners who support my efforts. This situation is not easy to get; I'm incredibly fortunate and don't want to waste this opportunity.

I live in a world in which I'm interdependent with all other sentient beings. In fact, I'm alive today due to the kindness and efforts of others: my parents who gave me this body, the farmers who have grown all the food I've eaten since I was born, and the teachers who taught me. All the abilities and talents I have are due to others who believed in me, who encouraged and taught me. All my possessions were made by others. I have been the recipient of an enormous amount of kindness in my life, and from the bottom of my heart I desire to give something back to the world and to help others find happiness.

The wonderful Buddha potential exists inside of me and I want to activate it. Through meditating, I will purify my harmful emotions, self-defeating habits, and negative karma. I will also nourish my good qualities. My deepest wish is to become a Buddha, a fully enlightened being, because as such I'll be able to contribute to the well-being of others most effectively. While on the path and after attaining enlightenment, my aim is to bring about the long-term happiness of all beings, myself included, to the best of my ability. This meditation session is helping me to grow in that direction.

The importance of having an expansive Dharma motivation cannot be emphasized enough. Not only does it determine the karmic or long-term effects of our actions, but also it gives meaning and purpose to our lives right now. It enables us to have joy and courage to continue practicing the Dharma. Over the years that I've been a monastic and Dharma student, I've noticed that the people who cultivate a long-term motivation are able to sustain their practices their entire lives. They remain peaceful even when they face difficulties that the rest of us would moan about. On the other hand, I've seen people who have excellent external conditions for practice, but cannot sustain their Dharma practice. Most of them seem to have weak long-term motivations. Perhaps they began by being inspired by a determination to be free or bodhicitta, but over time they did not nourish that intention and so it gradually deteriorated. The eight worldly concerns—craving sense pleasures, possessions, praise, and a good reputation, as well as aversion to not getting these four—snuck back in. They lost their self-confidence and trust in the efficacy of the Dharma as old habits reasserted themselves. This is indeed sad. For this reason, continuously nurturing our positive intentions and respecting our spiritual aspirations are essential.

MINDFULNESS OF BREATHING

After cultivating your motivation, you may want to spend some time on mindfulness of breathing. The instructions of this meditation are in the next chapter. Most Tibetan teachers do not emphasize breathing meditation, saying that it is sufficient to observe twenty-one breaths at the beginning of a meditation session to calm the mind. They then recommend doing the meditation on the Buddha. However, I have found that for people from busy societies who have a lot of stress and whose minds are filled with thoughts and preconceptions, spending more time on mindfulness of breathing can be helpful. On the one hand, observing the breath helps to calm the mind. On the other, we observe clearly what interferes with a calm mind: our body aches and our mind is unruly with many thoughts, emotions, memories, and expectations parading through it at an amazing rate. This untamed mind and uncooperative body are our samsara—our cyclic existence. Recognizing this activates us to do something about it, and thus we come to understand the purpose and function of Dharma practice. Without having an awareness of what our current experience is in cyclic existence, doing tantric practices in which we visualize ourselves as a deity becomes confusing.

Each person may do mindfulness of breathing for as long as he or she feels is beneficial. After that, continue with the meditation on the Buddha, which contains the rest of the preparatory practices. After that, do a specific analytic meditation.

4. MINDFULNESS OF BREATHING

MEDITATING on the breath is a widespread and nondenominational practice; we need not adhere to specific philosophical tenets or religious beliefs to benefit from it. Many spiritual traditions, both Buddhist and non-Buddhist, teach meditation on the breath. The meditation taught below is one way of meditating with the breath as the meditation object. You may encounter other Buddhist teachers or Buddhist traditions that give different instructions. All are valid ways of doing mindfulness of breathing.

THE PRACTICE OF MINDFULNESS OF BREATHING

Breathe normally and naturally, without forcing the breath in any way. Focus on one of the following:

- the tip of the nose and upper lip and observe the sensation of the air as it goes in and out
- the abdomen, observing its rising and falling with each inhalation and exhalation
- on the general sensation of the breath flowing in and out of your body

Initially you may spend a few meditation sessions experimenting to see which of the three methods works best for you. After you do, stay with that, without changing your focal point within a session or from one session to the next. At the beginning, some people find it useful to count each cycle of the breath, going from one to ten. Other people find this distracting. Check which is best for you.

While you observe your breath, let yourself be content. Our society has conditioned us to be dissatisfied with who we are, what we have, and what we do. We're usually thinking that we should be different than we are, have more than we have, and do something better than we're doing. Breathing meditation is a chance to be content with ourselves the way we are.

Contentment is the real richness. Practice letting yourself be content. If thoughts to the contrary arise, let them go. Think, "What I am is good enough. What I'm doing is good enough. What I have is good enough." As you retrain your mind to think in this way, you'll be more satisfied. Things will advance by themselves. You don't need to push in your life. Relax and enjoy the present moment in which you're living; it is the only moment you have.

As you become skilled in this meditation, gradually expand your awareness to be mindful not only of the sensation of the breath, but also of:

- the stages of the breath: Be aware of what it feels like when you're about to inhale, while you're inhaling, and when the inhalation is finishing. Be aware when you're about to exhale, while you're exhaling, and when the exhalation is finishing. If there is a natural pause, be aware of the sensations at that time. Be in the present, with the breath.
- the different kinds of breath: Notice when your breaths are long or short, when they are coarse (heavy) or fine (light), when they are rough or smooth.
- the relationship between the breath and your body. Is your body more or less comfortable and relaxed when the breath is long or short, rough or smooth?
- the relationship between the breath and your mental and emotional states. How do the feeling tones of the mind differ when the breath is long or short, rough or smooth? Do certain breathing patterns correspond to specific emotions?

How do the breath and various emotions and feelings of happiness or unhappiness affect each other? Here you may experiment, gently lengthening the inhalation and exhalation. How does this affect your emotions and thoughts?

- the changing nature, or impermanence, of the breath. Be aware of the change that is occurring in the breath, in the body, and in the mind moment by moment.

- whether or not there is a solid, independent person who is breathing or who is controlling the breath: Who is breathing? What is a breath? On what basis is it said, "I am breathing?"

The Buddha explained mindfulness of breathing in the *Foundations of Mindfulness Sutta (Satipatthana Sutta)* and in the *Mindfulness of Breathing Sutta (Anapanasati Sutta)*. You may wish to refer to those suttas (sutras) or to teachings on them for more information.

A SIDE BENEFIT

Calming our mind is not the only purpose of mindfulness of breathing. In fact, when properly done, the complete practice of mindfulness of breathing brings insight into the nature of reality. One immediate result of mindfulness of breathing is that we will clearly notice the objects, emotions, and thoughts that frequently occupy our mind. While we try to keep our attention on the breath, the mind continually runs off to other objects. At first we may be shocked at how uncontrolled and distracted our mind is or at the types of thoughts and emotions that arise in it. Some people may think that meditation is making their mind more undisciplined. However, this is not the case. Rather, our mind is usually filled with these same thoughts, emotions, and feelings, but because we are so busy going here and there and doing this and that, we have never noticed this. We are fortunate now to become aware of the contents of our mind. With that knowledge we will be able to change the aspects that lead to misery and confusion in our lives.

Being aware of the various thoughts and emotions that flit through, and sometimes overwhelm, the mind is the foundation for discerning constructive and destructive emotions and thoughts. We may intellectually know the definitions of these mental factors, but being able to observe them in our own experience is different. Once we are able to discern them and understand their causes, functions, and results, our motivation to counteract them using the antidotes the Buddha taught will increase. The chief mental afflictions, their disadvantages, and their antidotes are described in the chapter "Antidotes to the Mental Afflictions." The five hindrances and five faults that interfere with the development of serenity and their antidotes are discussed in the chapter "Working with Distractions."

ALTERNATIVES

In the context of meditating on the gradual path, mindfulness of breathing is done as a preliminary meditation, mainly for the purpose of calming the mind and subduing distracting thoughts, and the majority of the session involves analytical, or checking, meditation on a specific lamrim topic. As noted above, in other contexts an entire meditation session may be done using mindfulness of breathing. In addition, there are meditation objects other than the breath that may be used for calming the mind and cultivating concentration, if that is the focus of your meditation session.

While the breath works well for some people as the object of meditation when cultivating concentration or serenity, for others it doesn't. For example, some people who have asthma find observing the breath makes their mind tight. People who have bad allergies often cannot breathe through their nose, so following the breath is difficult. Fortunately, the Buddha taught a number of other meditation objects that can be used to develop concentration, such as loving-kindness, the parts of the body, and so forth. Describing all of these is beyond the scope of this book, but one that is commonly used in the Tibetan tradition is the visualized image of the Buddha.

Here we do not try to see the Buddha with our eyes, but instead see him in our "mind's eye." Imagine Shakyamuni Buddha appearing instantly in the space in front of you. He is the size of your thumb; visualizing a small image like this helps to focus the mind and prevents distraction. You may want to look at a statue or painting of the Buddha before your meditation session in order to remember his features, but in your session, lower your eyes and let the image of the Buddha arise in your mind. Going over all the details individually in your mind's eye helps you to remember them. After doing that, focus on the entire image. Be satisfied with the clarity of the image that appears, without making your mind tight in an effort to reconstruct each and every detail. If the clarity declines, review the Buddha's features and again focus your mind on the entire image. If the stability of your concentration is interrupted by thoughts and sensations, bring your mind back to the image of the Buddha.

Using the image of the Buddha as the meditation object to develop mindfulness and concentration has several unique advantages: it helps us to remember the Buddha continually and thus to accumulate positive potential and increase our feeling of connection to him. When death approaches, it will be easier to recollect the Buddha and his qualities, which will soothe the mind and maintain it in a positive state during the death process. It also increases our ability to visualize, which is helpful in other meditation practices in the Tibetan tradition.

5. Enjoying the Meditation Practices

Enjoying the meditation practices makes it easy to keep doing them. The more we are familiar with the practices and how to do them, the more enjoyable they will become. This chapter focuses on the meditation on the Buddha and lamrim analytical meditation in particular. An essential ingredient for enjoying Dharma practice is joyous effort, a mind that takes delight in virtue. There is no substitute for joyous effort, because it is our mind that can make any activity enjoyable or miserable.

Meditation on the Buddha

The next part of the meditation session is the meditation on the Buddha, which contains the rest of the preparatory practices that are good to do before meditating on the gradual path. The text for this and a detailed explanation of it appear in the chapter "Meditation on the Buddha" and track 2 of the CD. Shakyamuni Buddha is our fundamental teacher, and all the teachings we practice originate with him. Doing this meditation, in which we visualize the Buddha, purify, and accumulate positive potential, helps us form a close relationship to the Enlightened One. Imagining receiving the Buddha's blessings and inspiration increases our confidence and joy.

However, if you prefer to do the Je Tsongkhapa Guru Yoga, Chenrezig, or Tara practice, or another short *sadhana* (the text for meditation on a deity), that is fine, because they all follow the same basic outline.

The great masters of the past wrote these various meditation texts in order to help us cultivate positive attitudes that are conducive for deeper meditation. We beginners are not always capable of discerning the difference between wholesome thoughts and emotions and unwholesome ones. We may be ignorant of what to cultivate and what to abandon in order to progress on the path. Reading or reciting these prayers directs our mind in a beneficial way and contemplating their meaning transforms our mental state.

To summarize the main steps in the meditation on the Buddha: Think of all enlightened qualities manifesting as the Buddha, whom you visualize in the space in front of you. He is surrounded by other Buddhas and bodhisattvas, and you are surrounded by all sentient beings. To confirm your spiritual direction and your motivation for doing so, take refuge and generate bodhicitta. Then recite and contemplate the four immeasurables to deepen your love, compassion, joy, and equanimity for all sentient beings. Contemplating the seven-limb prayer purifies your mind of negative karmic latencies and creates positive potential by generating wholesome attitudes. As a result, understanding and gaining experience of the Dharma will be easier.

Next, with an attitude that sincerely seeks to actualize the path to enlightenment, offer the universe and everything beautiful in it—a practice called the mandala offering. Then request inspiration from the Buddha, verbalizing your respect and admiration for the qualities of the holy beings. This increases your feeling of connection to them and boosts your aspiration to generate those same qualities. The Buddha responds to your request for inspiration and blessings by emanating brilliant, soothing light that flows into you. Continue this visualization, letting the Buddha's wisdom and compassion in the form of beautiful light fill every part of your body and mind while you recite the Buddha's mantra: *tayata om muni muni maha muniye soha.*

You may then wish to do a glance meditation by reciting a short text such as "The Three Principal Aspects of the Path" or "The Foundation of All Good Qualities" to review the major steps of the gradual path. Doing this refreshes the meaning of each topic in your mind. It also plants the seeds of the realizations in your mind and thus sets the stage for deeper meditation on the topics. After that, meditate on a specific topic from the gradual path.

MEDITATION ON THE LAMRIM (GRADUAL PATH TO ENLIGHTENMENT)

Some people enjoy doing visualization practices and, feeling peaceful after this, they may end their meditation session at this point. If they do so, they miss an important opportunity to deepen their Dharma understanding by meditating on the gradual path. His Holiness the Dalai Lama and other masters continually stress the importance of doing analytical (checking) meditation on lamrim topics in order to integrate the meaning of the Dharma with our hearts and in our lives. From my own experience, I know that these meditations can have a profound effect on the way I view life and how I relate to others and the world around me. Unfortunately, nowadays some people think it's sufficient to listen to lamrim teachings and then go straight into tantric practice in which they visualize Buddhist deities and recite mantras. However, lacking lamrim realizations cripples one's tantric practice. Without renunciation and bodhicitta, we may do tantric meditations but our motivation will not be correct. Without understanding emptiness, we may visualize ourselves as a deity, but the self-grasping ignorance will remain unscathed.

Through meditating on the gradual path, we learn how to think properly. This is essential since our present way of thinking is often narrow, egotistical, or illogical. Some people mistakenly believe that the purpose of meditation is to stop all thoughts, when actually what we need to learn at the beginning of our spiritual practice is how to let go of distracting thoughts and cultivate the correct view. Because language is involved, conceptual thought has to be used in order to learn the Dharma teachings and to investigate and understand them correctly. Then, we develop meditative abilities that go beyond thought to nonconceptual experience and direct knowledge.

Using the CD of the guided meditations on the lamrim enables you to hear each point of a meditation and contemplate it without having to open your eyes to read the next point. If you want more time to meditate on a particular point, press the pause button. After a while, you will become so fluent with the steps of the meditations that you will no longer need to listen to the points or read them during your meditation sessions. An outline that follows the meditations on the CD can be found in the chapter "Lamrim Meditation Outlines." You may also want to refer to a lamrim outline in books on that topic. Making your own meditation outline after listening to oral teachings or reading a lamrim text is helpful for understanding the teachings.

If you are leading a lamrim meditation with a group, describe the first point and then leave a few minutes of silence so that the people in the group can meditate. After that, mention the next point and leave time for them to think about it. Whichever outline you use, contemplate each point fully by bringing in material that you have heard or read from different sources.

It is very important to think about all of these topics in terms of your own life. Simply reciting the points or intellectualizing about them does not transform your mind or bring deep meditative experience. Try to contemplate the meaning of the various points. For example, in the meditation on precious human life consider, "What would it be like if I were born as an animal, let's say as a fish? Would I be able to practice the Dharma? It's hard for a fish to listen to teachings or to reflect on their meaning, let alone to meditate on them."

When you begin to reflect on being born as another type of living being, let's say an animal, a hungry ghost, or a celestial being, doubt may arise, "I'm not sure I believe that other realms exist." Investigate this more deeply. Ask yourself, "Animals exist; what proof do I have that other life forms do not exist? What reasons are there to believe in rebirth? Are there reasons that disprove rebirth? I say I want someone to prove rebirth to me, but what kind of evidence or logical argument would actually satisfy me? If I believed in rebirth, how would that change my view of my life?" In other words, deeply think about the teachings. Check them using reasoning. Evaluate them according to what you have witnessed in the lives of others around you. Apply them to your own life, feelings, and relationships.

For example, in the meditation on precious human life, if rebirth already makes sense to you, then apply these points to your experience, thinking, "I haven't always been a human being living on this earth. In a previous life I might have been born as somebody else. In a future life, I will be different too. If I'm an animal, could I practice the Dharma? If I were born in the war zone in Iraq or starving in Darfur, would I be able to hear Dharma teachings and practice them? If I had a terrible physical or mental illness, how would that affect my ability to meet qualified teachers and have conducive circumstances to practice? If I lived in a place where there was no religious freedom, how would that influence by ability to practice the Dharma?"

Think about these things in a very personal way. In this way you will come to appreciate your present situation. You will feel tremendous gratitude, without any arrogance at all, because you see how easily you could have been born in another situation. You will feel energized to practice in order to make good use of the precious opportunity you have for spiritual transformation.

Similarly, when meditating on death, do not intellectually recite to yourself, "Yes, everybody dies. Hmm, I wonder what's for lunch?" Really contemplate, "I'm going to die. I have no choice about that, and I don't know when death will occur. It may be today." What impact does it have on your life when the fact that you won't live forever hits home? What is important when you die? Is what you are doing today going to be of benefit when you die? Are you prepared to separate from your body, your loved ones, and your ego identity at the time of death?

When meditating on karma (volitional actions), review the ten nonvirtues and the ten virtues. Contemplate, "When have I taken life and why? What was going on in my mind at that time? When have I protected life? Why is that important? How can I do that more?" Or look at how you have used your sexuality: "What does it mean to use sexuality wisely and kindly? Do I do that?" Apply the points in the meditation outline to your own life, making them very personal. This is of crucial importance for the success of these analytic meditations. If you just think about them intellectually, you will become bored and your mind will not be transformed. You will keep thinking, saying, and doing the same foolish or mindless activities that you did before. If you relate these meditations to your life, some strong experiences will ensue. These meditations will give you insight into your life and how your mind works. They will help you make wise decisions in the future, so that what you think, feel, say, and do will accord with the path to enlightenment.

Of course, these topics "push our buttons" and sometimes we don't like to think about them. Our ego mind would rather feel pleasure. Of course, there's nothing wrong with feeling good during meditation, but when we avoid meditations that make us examine our behavior and instead meditate with the same intention with which we do almost everything else in our life—the motivation to feel good now— then are we actually practicing the Dharma? Is our mind being transformed into virtue?

The purpose of meditation isn't to get a "hit" of good feeling. The purpose is to understand what life is about and how to make our lives meaningful. The purpose is to understand our Buddha potential and to actualize it for the benefit of all sentient beings. Make sure your motivation is suitable; try to understand the Buddha's teachings and apply them to your life because doing so will bring about enduring and beneficial change.

Be brave and honestly acknowledge what is going on in your mind. For example, let's say you do the meditation on equanimity, visualizing a friend, stranger, and enemy in front of you and examining, "Why am I attached to my friend? Why am I apathetic to the stranger? Why am I hostile towards the enemy?" Do research in the "laboratory" of your own mind and heart. In the process, you may discover some biases and prejudices. It may become evident how you create the friend and the enemy and ignore everybody who doesn't directly affect you.

We like to think we're broad-minded, caring people and realizing anything contrary to that may be difficult. Our self-centered attitude prefers to think, "I'm a really good person. I'm unhappy because the rest of the world is ignorant and hostile." As long as we hold that idea, spiritual progress will be difficult. As long as we keep blaming our problems on others and seek a "feel-good hit," we are not doing actual Dharma practice.

When doing lamrim meditations, it is important to know clearly the state of mind you want to reach as a conclusion to the meditation. Lamrim texts describe the purpose of each meditation, and we want to make sure that our mind arrives at that conclusion and not at an incorrect or irrelevant conclusion. For example, when meditating on the disadvantages of the self-centered thought, our mind may twist that meditation and conclude, "I'm a horrible person because I'm so selfish." This is the wrong conclusion to reach from that meditation. The Buddha didn't teach the disadvantages of self-centeredness so that we would deride ourselves.

If you meditate on a lamrim topic and arrive at an incorrect conclusion, the meditation hasn't been done correctly. In the above case, thinking, "I'm a bad person because I'm so selfish," indicates that we have misunderstood the purpose of the meditation and probably have fallen into an old pattern of putting ourselves down. Stop and ask yourself, "What conclusion does the Buddha want me to reach from this meditation? He wants me to ascertain that the self-centered mind is the actual 'enemy' that destroys my happiness. Self-centeredness is not an intrinsic part of me; it is not who I am. It's an incorrect, but deeply entrenched, thought that creates problems for me. I can free myself from it. Since I want to be happy, I will realize this selfish attitude for what it is and will stop following it! Instead, I will cultivate love and compassion for all beings." This is the conclusion you want to reach.

Listen to oral teachings, read books about the gradual path, and study texts about thought transformation to learn more about the self-centered mind. Then you will be able to recognize it correctly and not confuse it with the sense of self that is suitable and necessary on the path. Studying the lamrim will also enable you to learn the antidotes to counteract the self-centered attitude.

There are various ways in which you can cover all the lamrim topics over a period of time. You can do one lamrim topic each day, in sequence, until you reach the end and then start over again. In this way, you keep cycling through the meditations. Each time you do so, the insights you have into the former topics will deepen your meditation on the latter ones, and the insights you have into the latter topics will inform your reflections on the former ones. For example, meditating on your precious human life will inspire you to use it to cultivate the six far-reaching practices (*paramitas*) of generosity, ethical conduct, patience, joyous effort, concentration, and wisdom. In addition, reflecting on the six far-reaching practices gives you a deeper feeling about the preciousness and meaning of your present human life.

Another way to practice the gradual path is to put more attention on the beginning meditations and do the later topics more quickly. For example, reflect on your precious human life until you have a deep experience of it. Then reflect on its purpose. When your feeling for those topics is firm, go on to the rarity and causes of a precious human life. Stay with each topic as long as you need to in order to stabilize an experience of it before moving on to the next topic, but continue to review the preceding ones in order to maintain your feeling for them.

At the end of a lamrim meditation, dedicate the positive potential for the enlightenment of all living beings. This helps to protect the positive potential you created so that it won't be destroyed or hampered should anger or distorted views later arise in your mind. Dedication also steers our positive potential so that it will ripen in the long-term goal of enlightenment, instead of ripening simply on some brief pleasure while in cyclic existence. Since attaining enlightenment is predicated on having good circumstances for Dharma practice while we are still in cyclic existence, dedicating our practice towards the goal of enlightenment will also ripen in terms of having these fortunate circumstances.

PART II

The Meditations

6. MEDITATION ON THE BUDDHA

BEGIN by observing your breath for a few minutes to calm the mind. Think of the qualities of infinite love, compassion, wisdom, skillful means, and other wonderful qualities you aspire to develop. What would it feel like to have those qualities? Get a sense of the expansiveness and peace of having a wise and kind heart that reaches out impartially to work for the benefit of all beings.

Those qualities of love, compassion, wisdom, skillful means, and so on now appear in the physical form of the Buddha, in the space in front of you. He sits on an open lotus flower, and flat sun and moon disks. His body is made of radiant, transparent light, as is the entire visualization. His body is golden and he wears the robes of a monk. His right palm rests on his right knee and his left is in his lap, holding a bowl of nectar, which is medicine to cure our afflictions and other hindrances. The Buddha's face is very beautiful. His smiling, compassionate gaze looks at you with total acceptance and simultaneously encompasses all sentient beings. His eyes are long, narrow, and peaceful. His lips are red and his earlobes long.

Rays of light emanate from each pore of the Buddha's body and reach every part of the universe. These rays carry countless miniature Buddhas, some going out to help beings, others dissolving back into the Buddha after having finished their work.

The Buddha is surrounded by the entire lineage of spiritual teachers, all meditational deities, innumerable other Buddhas, bodhisattvas, arhats, dakas, dakinis, and Dharma protectors. To the side of each spiritual master is an elegant table upon which are arranged volumes of Dharma teachings.

Surrounding you are all sentient beings appearing in human form, with your mother on your left and your father on your right. The people you do not get along with are in front of you. All of you are looking to the Buddha for guidance.

Refuge and Bodhicitta

To cultivate a sense of refuge, first think of the dangers of cyclic existence by remembering your own dissatisfaction, suffering, and lack of security. Then think of all other sentient beings who, like you, flounder in cyclic existence, and generate compassion for them. Finally, think of the wonderful qualities of the Buddhas, Dharma, and Sangha, and generate confidence in their ability to guide you from the constantly recurring problems of cyclic existence. Since your present life provides the opportunity to free yourself from all these undesirable experiences, resolve to explore the path to enlightenment fully. Feel great trust and confidence in the Three Jewels and open your heart to rely on them to guide you and others from the torments of cyclic existence to the peace of liberation and enlightenment.

As you take refuge, imagine leading all the sentient beings around you in going for refuge to the Three Jewels. Visualize radiant light flowing from the spiritual mentors, Buddhas, bodhisattvas, and other holy beings into you and into all the beings around you, completely purifying all negative karmic latencies and afflictions. The light also enriches you with all the wondrous qualities and realizations of the path.

Namo Gurubhya.
Namo Buddhaya.
Namo Dharmaya.
Namo Sanghaya. (3x or 7x)

Feel that you and all others have come under the protection of the Three Jewels.

Now turn your thoughts to others and contemplate how much we depend on them for everything we enjoy and know in our lives. Our food, clothing, and everything we use and enjoy come due to their efforts. Similarly, our knowledge, talents, and good qualities have been developed due to the kindness of others. Even our ability to practice the Dharma and gain realizations depends on the kindness of sentient beings.

Just as your innermost wish is to be free from suffering and to abide in happiness, so too is it the aspiration of all other beings. But, they, like you, encounter sufferings and problems in their lives, and often their difficulties are much worse than your own.

Examine your capacity to help them. At this time your ability to help them is quite limited, but if you reduce your own ignorance, anger, attachment, and other faults, and increase your good qualities such as generosity, patience, loving-kindness, compassion, and wisdom, you will be of greater benefit. If you become fully enlightened, you will be of the greatest possible benefit to all beings. Thus generate the altruistic intention to become a Buddha in order to benefit all sentient beings most effectively. As you recite the refuge and bodhicitta prayer, much light flows from the Buddhas and other holy beings into you and all other sentient beings around you, purifying and enriching your minds.

> I take refuge until I am enlightened in the Buddhas, the Dharma, and the Sangha. By the positive potential I create by practicing generosity and the other far-reaching attitudes, may I attain Buddhahood in order to benefit all sentient beings. (3x)

The Buddha is extremely pleased with your altruistic intention. A replica emerges from him and goes to the crown of your head. He melts into golden, radiant light that flows into you, and you and the Buddha become inseparable. Feel close to the Buddha, and feel that your mind has been inspired and transformed.

Let go of all conceptions you have about yourself, particularly any self-denigrating thoughts and the concept of inherent existence, and meditate on emptiness. (Meditate)

At your heart appears a small Buddha made of light. He radiates the light of wisdom and compassion in all directions, throughout the entire universe. The light transforms all sentient beings into Buddhas and transforms all environments into pure lands—places with all conducive circumstances for practicing the Dharma and generating realizations of the path. (Meditate)

You have transformed all sentient beings and their environments into enlightened beings and pure lands in your imagination. Why hasn't this become a reality? Because we sentient beings have bias and prejudice, and lack love, compassion, and joy. Wishing yourself and others to have these, contemplate the four immeasurables. Reinforce your feelings of love, compassion, joy, and equanimity for everyone— friends, relatives, strangers, as well as those whom you dislike, mistrust, disapprove of, and those who have harmed you in the past.

> May all sentient beings have happiness and its causes.
> May all sentient beings be free of suffering and its causes.
> May all sentient beings not be separated from sorrowless bliss.
> May all sentient beings abide in equanimity, free of bias, attachment,
>   and anger.

Seven-limb Prayer

Now offer the seven-limb prayer to purify negativities and create positive potential.

> Reverently I prostrate with my body, speech, and mind,

Imagine you and sentient beings throughout infinite space bow to the field of positive potential.

> And present clouds of every type of offering, actual and mentally
>   transformed.

Imagine every beautiful object you can and offer it to the field of positive potential. Imagine the sky filled with lovely offerings, and offer them. Similarly, think of everything and everyone to whom you are attached, and offer them to the field of positive potential as well.

I confess all my negative actions accumulated since beginningless time,

Acknowledge your past mistakes and harmful actions and purify them by contemplating the four opponent powers: 1) regret, 2) taking refuge and generating bodhicitta, 3) determining not to do them again, and 4) engaging in a remedial action.

And rejoice in the virtues of all holy and ordinary beings.

Think of the virtues of all the holy and ordinary beings and feel happy. Abandon any feeling of jealousy or envy and rejoice in all the goodness in the world.

Please remain until cyclic existence ends,

Offer a double *dorje*, symbolizing long life, to the members of the field of positive potential, and request them to live long and always be part of your life.

And turn the wheel of Dharma for sentient beings.

Offer a thousand-spoked Dharma wheel to the field of positive potential, requesting them to teach the Dharma and to guide you in your practice.

I dedicate all the virtues of myself and others to the great enlightenment.

Rejoicing at your own and others' positive potential, dedicate it to the enlightenment of yourself and all sentient beings.

MANDALA OFFERING

With the wish to offer everything in the universe in order to receive Dharma teachings and to realize them in your mindstream, imagine the entire universe and everything beautiful in it, and respectfully offer it to the field of positive potential.

> This ground, anointed with perfume, flowers strewn,
> Mount Meru, four lands, sun and moon,
> Imagined as a Buddha land and offered to you.
> May all beings enjoy this pure land.

> The objects of attachment, aversion, and ignorance—friends, enemies,
> and strangers, my body, wealth, and enjoyments—I offer these without any
> sense of loss. Please accept them with pleasure, and inspire me and others to
> be free from the three poisonous attitudes.

> Idam guru ratna mandala kam nirya tayami.

All the beings in the field of positive potential receive your offerings with delight. The offerings dissolve into light and absorb into the Buddha's heart. From his heart, light radiates to you, filling your body and mind, and inspiring you to accomplish the path.

REQUESTING INSPIRATION

To progress on the path and develop the realizations of the path to enlightenment, you need the inspiration of the lineage of spiritual masters, especially your principal teacher or root guru, the one who touched your heart so deeply with the Dharma. Thus request:

Glorious and precious root guru, sit upon the lotus and moon seat on my crown. Guiding me with your great kindness, bestow upon me the attainments of your body, speech, and mind.

A replica of your teacher, in the aspect of the Buddha, emerges from the Buddha in front of you and comes to sit on a lotus and moon cushion on your head, facing the same direction as you. The Buddha on your crown acts as an advocate for you in requesting inspiration from the entire field of positive potential as you make request to the lineage teachers:

Buddha, unequalled teacher and guide; Venerable protector Maitreya, his successor; Superior Asanga, prophesied by Buddha; to you three Buddhas and bodhisattvas I make request.

Buddha, head of the Shakya clan, the foremost guide, peerless in expounding emptiness; Manjushri, embodiment of the Buddha's complete wisdom; exalted Nagarjuna, best of the Superiors who sees the profound meaning; to you three crowning jewels of clear exposition I make request.

Atisha, upholder of this great vehicle, who sees the profundity of dependent arising; Drom Rinpoche, elucidator of this good path; to these two ornaments of the world I make request.

Avalokiteshvara, great treasure of objectless compassion; Manjushri, master of flawless wisdom; Tsongkhapa, crown jewel of the Snowy Land's sages, Lobsang Drakpa, I make request at your feet.

Holder of the white lotus, embodiment of all the conquerors' compassion, guide benefiting migrating beings in the land of snow mountains and beyond, sole deity and refuge, Tenzin Gyatso, at your feet, I make request.

The eyes through whom the vast scriptures are seen, supreme doors for the fortunate who would cross over to spiritual freedom, illuminators whose wise means vibrate with compassion, to the entire line of spiritual masters I make request.

(Optional: Do a glance meditation on the stages of the path by reciting "The Foundation of All Good Qualities" or "The Three Principal Aspects of the Path." If you prefer, the glance meditation may be done after reciting the Buddha's mantra below.)

All the figures in the field of positive potential melt into light and dissolve into the central figure of the Buddha in front of you. As the embodiment of the Three Jewels, the Buddha now absorbs into the Buddha on your crown. As you recite the Buddha's mantra, much white light flows from the Buddha into you, purifying all negativities and obscurations and generating within you all the realizations of the gradual path.

Tayata om muni muni maha muniye soha. (at least 21x)

MEDITATION ON THE GRADUAL PATH

Now do one of the analytical meditations of the gradual path.

ABSORPTION

At the conclusion of your meditation, the Buddha on your head melts into light and dissolves into you. Your body, speech, and mind become inseparable from those of the Buddha. (Meditate)

DEDICATION

Due to this merit may we soon
Attain the enlightened state of Guru Buddha,
That we may be able to liberate
All sentient beings from their sufferings.

May the precious bodhi mind
Not yet born arise and grow.
May that born have no decline,
But increase forever more.

In the snowy mountain paradise
You're the source of good and happiness,
Powerful Tenzin Gyatso Chenrezig,
May you stay until samsara ends.

7. Recitations before Meditation Sessions

Some days you may wish to do a shortened version of the meditation on the Buddha. In this case, visualize the Buddha in front of you and recite the following verses while contemplating their meaning:

Refuge

Namo Gurubhya.
Namo Buddhaya.
Namo Dharmaya.
Namo Sanghaya. (3x or 7x)

Refuge and Generating the Altruistic Intention

I take refuge until I am enlightened in the Buddhas, the Dharma, and the Sangha. By the positive potential I create by practicing generosity and the other far-reaching attitudes, may I attain Buddhahood in order to benefit all sentient beings. (3x)

Four Immeasurables

May all sentient beings have happiness and its causes.

May all sentient beings be free of suffering and its causes.

May all sentient beings not be separated from sorrowless bliss.

May all sentient beings abide in equanimity, free of bias, attachment, and anger.

Seven-limb Prayer

Reverently I prostrate with my body, speech, and mind,

And present clouds of every type of offering, actual and mentally transformed.

I confess all my negative actions accumulated since beginningless time,

And rejoice in the virtues of all holy and ordinary beings.

Please remain until cyclic existence ends,

And turn the wheel of Dharma for sentient beings.

I dedicate all the virtues of myself and others to the great enlightenment.

Mandala Offering

This ground, anointed with perfume, flowers strewn,

Mount Meru, four lands, sun and moon,

Imagined as a Buddha land and offered to you.

May all beings enjoy this pure land.

The objects of attachment, aversion, and ignorance—friends, enemies, and strangers, my body, wealth, and enjoyments—I offer these without any sense of loss. Please accept them with pleasure, and inspire me and others to be free from the three poisonous attitudes.

Idam guru ratna mandala kam nirya tayami.

Requesting Inspiration

Glorious and precious root guru, sit upon the lotus and moon seat on my crown. Guiding me with your great kindness, bestow upon me the attainments of your body, speech, and mind.

The eyes through whom the vast scriptures are seen, supreme doors for the fortunate who would cross over to spiritual freedom, illuminators whose wise means vibrate with compassion, to the entire line of spiritual masters I make request.

Shakyamuni Buddha's Mantra

Tayata om muni muni maha muniye soha. (3x or 7x)

Meditation

Now do one of the lamrim meditations. At the end of your session, recite:

Dedication of Positive Potential

Due to this merit may we soon
Attain the enlightened state of Guru Buddha,
That we may be able to liberate
All sentient beings from their sufferings.

May the precious bodhi mind
Not yet born arise and grow.
May that born have no decline,
But increase forever more.

LONG LIFE PRAYER FOR HIS HOLINESS THE DALAI LAMA

In the snowy mountain paradise
You're the source of good and happiness,
Powerful Tenzin Gyatso Chenrezig,
May you stay until samsara ends.

8. The Foundation of All Good Qualities

by Je Tsongkhapa

THE KIND and venerable spiritual master is the foundation of all good qualities. Seeing that dependence on him or her is the root of the path, may I rely on him or her with great respect and continuous effort—inspire me thus!

A human life with leisure is obtained this once. Understanding that it has great value and is hard to find, may I produce unceasingly the mind that takes hold of its essence day and night—inspire me thus!

The fluctuation of our body and life is like a bubble of water; remember death, for we perish so quickly. After death, the effects of black and white karma pursue us as a shadow follows a body. Finding certainty in this, may I always be careful to abandon even the slightest negative action and to complete the accumulation of virtue—inspire me thus!

There is no satisfaction in enjoying worldly pleasures. They are the door to all misery. Having realized that the fault of samsaric perfections is that they cannot be trusted, may I be strongly intent on the bliss of liberation—inspire me thus!

That pure thought (to attain liberation) produces great conscientiousness, mindfulness, and awareness. May I make the essential practice keeping the vows of individual liberation, the root of the doctrine—inspire me thus!

Having seen that all beings, my kind mothers, have fallen like myself into the ocean of cyclic existence, may I train in the supreme altruistic intention, assuming the responsibility to free all migrating beings—inspire me thus!

Generating the altruistic intention alone, without cultivation of the three ethical practices, does not lead to enlightenment. Having realized this, may I practice with intense effort the vows of the conquerors and their spiritual children—inspire me thus!

By quieting distraction to false objects, and analyzing the meaning of reality, may I quickly generate within my mindstream the path uniting serenity and special insight—inspire me thus!

When, trained in the common path, I am a suitable vessel, let me enter with ease the great gateway of the fortunate ones, the Vajrayana, the highest of all vehicles—inspire me thus!

The basis of achieving the two powerful attainments is the pure vows and commitments that I have pledged. Having found true understanding of this, may I keep them even at the cost of my life—inspire me thus!

Having realized the significance of the two stages, which are the essence of the tantric path, may I steadfastly practice without laziness the four sessions of yoga, and realize what the holy beings have taught—inspire me thus!

May the spiritual teachers who lead me on the sacred path and all spiritual friends who practice it have long life. May I quickly and completely pacify all outer and inner hindrances—grant such inspiration, I pray!

In all my rebirths may I never be separated from perfect spiritual masters, and enjoy the magnificent Dharma. Completing all qualities of the stages and paths, may I quickly achieve the stage of Vajradhara.

9. The Three Principal Aspects of the Path

by Je Tsongkhapa

I BOW DOWN to the venerable spiritual masters.

I will explain, as well as I am able, the essence of all the teachings of the Conqueror, the path praised by the Conquerors and their spiritual children, the entrance for the fortunate ones who desire liberation.

Listen with clear minds, you fortunate ones who direct your minds to the path pleasing to the Buddha and strive to make good use of freedom and fortune without being attached to the joys of cyclic existence.

For you embodied beings bound by the craving for existence, without the pure determination to be free (renunciation) from the ocean of existence, there is no way for you to pacify the attractions to its pleasurable effects. Thus, from the outset seek to generate the determination to be free.

By contemplating the freedoms and fortunes so difficult to find and the fleeting nature of your life, reverse the clinging to this life. By repeatedly contemplating the infallible effects of karma and the miseries of cyclic existence, reverse the clinging to future lives.

By contemplating in this way, do not generate even for an instant the wish for the pleasures of cyclic existence. When you have, day and night unceasingly, the mind aspiring for liberation, you have generated the determination to be free.

However, if your determination to be free is not sustained by the pure altruistic intention (bodhicitta), it does not become the cause for the perfect bliss of unsurpassed enlightenment. Therefore, the intelligent generate the supreme thought of enlightenment.

Swept by the current of the four powerful rivers, tied by the strong bonds of karma which are so hard to undo, caught in the iron net of self-grasping egoism, completely enveloped by the darkness of ignorance, born and reborn in boundless cyclic existence, unceasingly tormented by the three sufferings—by thinking of all mother sentient beings in this condition, generate the supreme altruistic intention.

Even if you meditate upon the determination to be free and the altruistic intention, without the wisdom realizing the ultimate nature you cannot cut the root of cyclic existence. Therefore, strive for the means to realize dependent arising.

One who sees the infallible cause and effect of all phenomena in cyclic existence and beyond and destroys all false perceptions of their inherent existence has entered the path which pleases the Buddha.

Appearances are infallible dependent arisings; emptiness is free of assertions of inherent existence or nonexistence. As long as these two understandings are seen as separate, one has not yet realized the intent of the Buddha.

When these two realizations are simultaneous and concurrent, from the mere sight of infallible dependent arising comes definite knowledge which completely destroys all modes of mental grasping. At that time, the analysis of the profound view is complete.

In addition, appearances clear away the extreme of inherent existence; emptiness clears away the extreme of nonexistence. When you understand the arising of cause and effect from the viewpoint of emptiness, you are not captivated by either extreme view.

In this way, when you have realized the exact points of the three principal aspects of the path, by depending on solitude, generate the power of joyous effort and quickly accomplish the final goal, my spiritual child!

10. Lamrim Meditation Outlines

THE FOLLOWING MEDITATION outlines correspond to the guided meditations on the CD. Sometimes you may wish to do the meditation while listening to the CD, other times you may wish to guide yourself by following the outline. As you learn more about each topic in the gradual path through reading and attending Dharma talks, you may wish to jot down some notes or quotations to enrich your meditation on the various points. This chapter begins with a concise list of the meditations and is followed by the expanded points for each meditation on the gradual path.

INTRODUCTION TO THE BUDDHIST VIEW

- Mind Is the Source of Happiness and Pain
- Taking the Ache out of Attachment
- Transforming Attachment
- The Nature of Mind
- Mind and Rebirth
- The Four Noble Truths
- The Three Characteristics

THE PATH IN COMMON WITH THE INITIAL LEVEL PRACTITIONER

- Precious Human Life
- The Purpose and Opportunity of Our Precious Human Life
- The Rarity and Difficulty of Attaining a Precious Human Life
- The Eight Worldly Concerns
- The Nine-Point Death Meditation
- Imagining Our Death
- Refuge: Its Meaning, Causes, and Objects
- Refuge: An Analogy and the Qualities of the Three Jewels
- The Law of Karma and Its Effects
- The Ten Nonvirtues
- The Results of Karma
- The Four Opponent Powers for Purification
- Constructive Actions

THE PATH IN COMMON WITH THE MIDDLE LEVEL PRACTITIONER

- The Eight Sufferings of Human Beings
- The Six Difficulties of Cyclic Existence
- The Causes of Cyclic Existence
- Factors That Stimulate the Arising of Mental Afflictions
- The Paths That Cease the Disturbing Attitudes, Negative Emotions, and Karma

THE PATH OF THE ADVANCED PRACTITIONER

- Equanimity
- All Sentient Beings Have Been Our Parents, Their Kindness, and Repaying Their Kindness
- The Kindness of Others
- Equalizing Self and Others

- The Disadvantages of Self-Centeredness
- The Advantages of Cherishing Others
- Love
- Compassion
- Exchanging Self and Others
- Taking and Giving
- The Great Resolve and the Altruistic Intention (Bodhicitta)
- Far-Reaching Generosity
- Far-Reaching Ethical Conduct
- Far-Reaching Patience
  - The Disadvantages of Anger
  - The Antidotes to Anger
- Far-Reaching Joyous Effort
- Far-Reaching Concentration
- Far-Reaching Wisdom
  - Dependent Arising
  - Emptiness
- How to Rely on a Spiritual Mentor

INTRODUCTION TO THE BUDDHIST VIEW

Since many people now interested in Buddhism have not been raised Buddhist and have not lived in a Buddhist culture, some initial reflections on basic Buddhist approaches are helpful. The first three meditations help us understand how our mind operates in daily life and how our mental processes—our thoughts and feelings—influence our experiences.

MIND IS THE SOURCE OF HAPPINESS AND PAIN

Mind is the forerunner of all actions;
All deeds are led by mind, created by mind.
If one speaks or acts with a corrupt mind,
Suffering follows, as wheels follow the hoof of an ox.

Mind is the forerunner of all actions;
All deeds are led by mind, created by mind.
If one speaks or acts with a serene mind,
Happiness follows as surely as one's shadow.
Buddha, *The Dhammapada*

1. Remember a disturbing situation in your life. Recall what you were thinking and feeling (not what the other person was saying and doing). How did the way you described the situation to yourself influence how you experienced it?
2. Examine how your attitude affected what you said and did in the situation. How did your words and actions affect the situation? How did the other person respond to what you said and did?
3. Was your view of the situation realistic? Were you seeing all sides of the situation or were you seeing things through the eyes of "me, I, my, and mine?"
4. Think of how you could have viewed the situation differently if you had had a broad mind and been free from self-centeredness. How would that have changed your experience of it?

Conclusion: Determine to be aware of how you interpret events and to cultivate beneficial and realistic ways of looking at them.

Taking the Ache out of Attachment

> Attachment is no friend, but seems like one,
> Which is why you do not fear it.
> But shouldn't people particularly
> Rid themselves of a harmful friend?
> Aryadeva, *The Four Hundred*

Based on a superimposition or exaggeration of the positive qualities of a person, object, idea, etc., attachment is an attitude that clings to an object as the source of happiness. Attachment differs from positive aspiration. For example, being attached to money is different from having a positive aspiration to learn the Dharma. Reflect:

1. What things, people, places, ideas, etc. are you attached to? Make specific examples. _Children_
2. How does that person or thing appear to you? Does it really have all the qualities you perceive and attribute to it?
3. Do you develop unrealistic expectations of the person or thing, thinking that person or thing will always be there and will continuously make you happy?
4. How does your attachment make you act? For example, do you disregard your ethical standards to get what you're attached to? Do you get into dysfunctional relationships? Do you become manipulative or aggressive?

Conclusion: See attachment not as your friend bringing you happiness, but as a thief destroying your peace of mind. Recognizing the disadvantages of attachment helps to let go of it.

TRANSFORMING ATTACHMENT

> Attachment arises from (wrong) conceptions,
> So know them as attachment's root.
> Avoid conceptualizations,
> And then attachment will not arise
> > Buddha, *The Dhammapada*

Thinking of the object of your attachment, apply an antidote to attachment. Each of the four points below is a separate antidote. You can use an example from your life for each point.

1. If you possess this thing, person, etc., or if you get your way, will it bring lasting happiness and satisfaction? What new problems could arise? Does any external person or thing have the ability to bring you lasting happiness?
2. If you separate from this object or person, what is the worst thing that could happen? Is that likely to happen? What resources—internal and in the community—can help you deal with the situation?
3. Look back at the thing, person, etc. that you are now separated from and rejoice at the time you had together. Go into the future with optimism.
4. Imagine giving the thing or person to someone else who receives it with joy. With a joyful mind, imagine offering the thing or person to the Buddha.

Conclusion: Feel balanced and free to enjoy without clinging.

Having observed how our mind operates in daily life, let's now look at the mind itself—its nature and its continuity from life to life.

THE NATURE OF MIND

> This mind, O monastics, is luminous, but it is defiled by adventitious defilements. The uninstructed worldling does not understand this as it really is; therefore for him there is no mental development.

> This mind, O monastics, is luminous, and it is freed from adventitious defilements. The instructed noble disciple understands this as it really is; therefore for him there is mental development.
>
> Buddha, "The Mind II," *Anguttara Nikaya*

The word "mind" does not refer to the brain, because the brain is made of atoms while the mind is not. The mind is that part of us that experiences, feels, perceives, thinks, and so forth. The presence of the mind is what makes the difference between a living being and a dead body. The mind has two qualities: 1) clarity: it is formless and allows objects to arise in it, and 2) awareness: it can engage with objects.

Calm your mind by observing the breath. Then turn your attention to the mind itself, to what is meditating, experiencing, feeling; that is, to the subject, not object, of the meditation. Observe:

1. What is your mind? Does it have shape or color? Where is it? Can you find your mind somewhere?
2. Try to get a sense of the clarity and awareness that are perceiving, feeling, and experiencing.
3. Focus on the perceiving subject, not on the object of the perception. If thoughts arise, observe: What are thoughts? Where do they come from? Where are they? Where do they go when they cease?

Conclusion: Experience your mind as being clarity and awareness, free from thought.

MIND AND REBIRTH

Our present life is not an isolated, independent event, but part of a continuity. Although there is no soul or permanent self, our mindstream has existed before this life and will continue to exist in the future.

1. Are you the same person who was an infant and who will be an aged person, or are you in a state of constant flux? Recognize that your body and mind have changed from conception to the present and that they will continue to change in the future. In this way, loosen the concept that views yourself as permanent and the concept that identifies "I" with the present body and mind.
2. The body is material in nature. The mind is formless; it is clear and knowing. Thus the continuities of body and mind are different. Look at the qualities of your body and mind and see how they are different.
3. Rebirth can be explained in terms of cause and effect. Each moment of mind has a cause: the preceding moment of mind. Get a sense of the continuity of mind by going back in your life, noting that each moment of mind arose from the previous moment. When you get to the time of conception, ask, "Where did this moment of mind come from?"

Some other ways for getting a sense of rebirth are to:

1. Contemplate the stories of people who remember previous lives.
2. Provisionally accept rebirth. What other things could it help to explain, for example, déjà vu experiences, the differing personalities of children within the same family, and familiarity with certain skills or subjects?
3. Since your body—the life form you are born into—is a reflection of your mental states, consider that very pronounced mental states could cause rebirth in certain types of bodies. For example, a human being who acts worse than an animal could be reborn as an animal.

Conclusion: Feel that you are not simply this present person, but instead exist as part of a continuum that spans more than just this life.

The mind is clarity and awareness. It has a continuity that is beginningless and endless, taking rebirth in one body after another. Let's now examine the Four Noble Truths, which describe the unsatisfactory situation of uncontrolled rebirth in which we are presently caught, as well as our potential for liberation and happiness.

THE FOUR NOBLE TRUTHS

> Here a monastic understands as it actually is: "This is dukkha"; he understands as it actually is: "This is the origin of dukkha"; he understands as it actually is: "This is the cessation of dukkha"; he understands as it actually is: "This is the way leading to the cessation of dukkha."
>
> Buddha, *The Foundations of Mindfulness Sutta*

The first two of the Four Noble Truths outline our present situation and its causes; the last two present our potential and the path to actualize it.

1. It is true that we experience unsatisfactory conditions, suffering, difficulties, and problems. Suffering is to be recognized. What difficulties, both physical and mental, do you have in your life? See them as part of the human experience, as arising simply because you have the body and mind that you do.
2. It is true that these unsatisfactory experiences have causes: ignorance, attachment, anger, and other mental afflictions, as well as the actions (karma) we do under their influence. These causes of our unsatisfactory situation are to be abandoned.

Conclusion: See how your negative emotions cause you suffering and perpetuate the unsatisfactory state of cyclic existence in which you are caught. Reflect that these mental afflictions distort your perception of an object and cause you to act in ways that bring suffering to yourself and to others.

3. It is true that the possibility to cease completely these unsatisfactory conditions and their causes exists. These cessations are to be actualized. Reflect that it is possible to be free from mental afflictions, karma, and dukkha. What would it feel like not to be under the influence of disturbing attitudes, negative emotions, and the actions motivated by them?

4. It is true that there is a path to bring about this liberation. The path is to be practiced. Generate the aspiration to cultivate it.

Conclusion: True cessations and true paths are the Dharma refuge. Make a determination to abandon any chaotic or misinformed ways that falsely promise happiness and to follow the paths of ethical conduct, concentration, and wisdom, as well as to generate love, compassion, and bodhicitta.

THE THREE CHARACTERISTICS

Those who perceive the changing to be permanent,
Suffering (dukkha) as bliss, a self in the selfless,
And who see in the foul the mark of beauty—
Such folk resort to distorted views,
Mentally deranged, subject to illusions.
Caught by Mara, not free from bonds,
They are still far from the secure state.
Such beings wander through the painful round
And go repeatedly from birth to death.
But when the Buddhas appear in the world,
The makers of light in a mass of darkness,
They reveal this Teaching, the noble Dharma,
That leads to the end of suffering.

When people with wisdom listen to them,
They at last regain their sanity.
They see the impermanent as impermanent,
And they see suffering just as suffering.
They see the selfless as void of self,
And in the foul, they see the foul.
By this acceptance of right view,
They overcome all suffering.

          Buddha, "Distortions of Perceptions," *Anguttara Nikaya*

Contemplating the three characteristics of all things in cyclic existence helps us to better understand our present situation and potential. All people and things in cyclic existence have three characteristics:

1. transience or impermanence. By looking at your life, reflect:
   - Everything in our world—people, objects, reputation, etc.—is transient and changeable by its very nature.
   - Our refusal to accept this reality causes us pain.
   - In your heart, try to accept the transient nature of all things.
2. unsatisfactory conditions (dukkha). Not everything is one hundred percent wonderful in our lives. We experience:
   - unsatisfactory situations of pain and suffering, both physical and mental
   - happy situations that are unsatisfactory because they are actually no more than a temporary alleviation of suffering. In addition, they change and disappear.
   - the unsatisfactory situation of having a body that ages, gets sick, and dies, and a mind that is under the control of afflictions and karma
3. selflessness. Reflect that all these seemingly solid and independent things—ourselves and other phenomena—are without inherent, findable existence. Understanding this counteracts ignorance, thus eliminating the root cause of all the unsatisfactory experiences of cyclic existence.

Reflect on transience, unsatisfactory conditions, and selflessness and then remember your spiritual potential. Make a determination to let go of the clinging and ignorance that keep you bound to cyclic existence.

Having a general idea of the Buddhist approach, let's now begin the meditations of the three levels of practitioners: initial, middle, and advanced.

THE PATH IN COMMON WITH THE INITIAL LEVEL PRACTITIONER

An initial level practitioner contemplates death and impermanence and, as a result, generates the aspiration for a good rebirth. He or she then takes refuge and observes the law of karma and its effects in order to actualize that aspiration. In order to practice the path in common with the initial level practitioner, we must first reflect on our current human life, its meaning and purpose, and its rarity, so that we do not take our present opportunity for granted.

PRECIOUS HUMAN LIFE

> Human life plants the seed
> For going beyond cyclic existence,
> The supreme seed of glorious enlightenment.
> Human life is a stream of good qualities
> Better than a wish-granting jewel.
> Who here would attain it and then waste it?
> > Aryashura, *Talk Which Is Like a Jeweled Receptacle
> > of Good Explanations*

Check if you have conditions conducive for spiritual practice. Consider the advantage of each quality, rejoice if you have it, and think of how to gain it if you don't.

1. Are you free from unfortunate states? Do you have a human body and human intelligence?
2. Are your sense and mental faculties healthy and complete?
3. Do you live at a time when a Buddha has appeared and given teachings? Do those teachings still exist in a pure form? Do you live in a place where you have access to them?
4. Have you committed any of the five heinous actions (killing one's father, mother, or an arhat, drawing blood from a Buddha's body, or causing a schism in the sangha) which obscure the mind and make practice difficult?
5. Are you naturally interested in spiritual practice? Do you have instinctive belief in things worthy of respect, such as ethical conduct, the path to enlightenment, compassion, and the Dharma?
6. Do you have a supportive group of spiritual friends who encourage your practice and who act as good examples? Do you live near a sangha community of monks and nuns?
7. Do you have the material conditions for practice such as food, clothes, and so forth?
8. Do you have access to qualified spiritual teachers who can guide you along the correct path?

Conclusion: Feel like a beggar who just won the lottery, that is, feel joyful and enthusiastic about everything you have going for you in your life.

(Note: if you would like to do the full meditation on the precious human life as described in the lamrim texts, the outline is in Appendix 2.)

The Purpose and Opportunity of Our Precious Human Life

Having gained this rare ship of freedom and fortune,
Hear, think, and meditate unwaveringly night and day
In order to free yourself and others

From the ocean of cyclic existence—
This is the practice of bodhisattvas.
>   Gyelsay Togmay Sangpo, *The Thirty-seven Practices of Bodhisattvas*

1. What does it mean to you to live a meaningful life? To what extent are you doing that now? How could you make your life more meaningful?
2. Consider the purpose of having a precious human life:
   - temporary goals within cyclic existence. We have the ability to create the causes for happy rebirths in the future.
   - ultimate goals. We have the ability to attain liberation or enlightenment, that is, to be free of all problems and capable of helping others effectively.
   - We can make each moment of our lives meaningful, transforming it into the path to enlightenment by practicing thought training. We can generate bodhicitta each morning and remember it throughout the day as the motivation for everything we do.

Conclusion: Recognize that there are many beneficial things to do in life and be enthusiastic about doing them.

THE RARITY AND DIFFICULTY OF ATTAINING A PRECIOUS HUMAN LIFE

The leisure and endowment, which are so difficult to obtain, have been
>   acquired,
And they bring about the welfare of the world.
If one fails to take this favorable opportunity into consideration,
How could this occasion occur again?
>   Shantideva, *A Guide to the Bodhisattva's Way of Life*

To develop a sense of the value of your present life, consider:

1. The causes for a precious human life are:
   - keeping pure ethical conduct by abandoning the ten nonvirtues
   - practicing the six far-reaching attitudes (paramitas)
   - making pure prayers to be able to have a precious human life and practice the Dharma

   Examine the actions you and others do. Do most people create these causes each day? Is it easy to create the causes for a precious human life?

2. Attaining a precious human life in the ocean of cyclic existence is as likely as a blind tortoise, who comes to the ocean's surface once every hundred years, putting his head through a golden ring floating on the ocean's surface. How likely is this?

3. Are there more human beings or animals on this planet? Of those who are human, are there more who have precious human lives or more who do not? Looking at the numbers, is it rare or common to have a precious human life?

Conclusion: Feel amazed at your fortune to have this present opportunity and determine to use it well.

We are extremely fortunate to have a precious human life with its freedoms and fortunes. It is rare and difficult to attain and have great purpose and meaning. But, how much does this understanding influence our daily lives? Do we spend most of our time and energy cultivating our minds and hearts? Or, are we ruled by our attachment and anger, being tangled up in distractions, such as the eight worldly concerns, which seem important now, but in the long term are not? Let's look into this.

THE EIGHT WORLDLY CONCERNS

Loss and gain, disrepute and fame,
Praise and blame, pleasure and pain—
These things are transient in human life,
Inconstant and bound to change.

The mindful wise one discerns them well,
Observant of their alterations.
Pleasant things do not stir his mind
And those unpleasant do not annoy him.
All likes and dislikes are dispelled by him,
Eliminated and abolished.
Aware now of the stainless, griefless state (*nirvana*),
He fully knows, having gone beyond.
Buddha, "The Vicissitudes of Life," *Anguttara Nikaya*

The eight worldly concerns are the chief distractions to practicing the Dharma and transforming our minds. They can be grouped into four pairs:

1. attachment to receiving material possessions and aversion to not receiving them or to being separated from them
2. attachment to praise or approval and aversion to blame or disapproval
3. attachment to a good reputation (having a good image, others thinking well of you) and aversion to a bad reputation
4. attachment to pleasures of the five senses and aversion to unpleasant experiences

Examine how the four pairs of worldly concerns operate in your life:

1. Think of specific examples of each type of attachment and each type of aversion. Do they make you happy or confused? Do they help you to grow or do they keep you in prison?
2. Reflect that the more you are attached to someone or something, the more aversion you will have when you don't get it or are separated from that person or thing.
3. Apply some of the antidotes to attachment and anger in order to transform those attitudes.

Conclusion: Feel that you don't want to continue living your life on "automatic" and that you want to change the attitudes that cause you to have problems.

The eight worldly concerns dominate our lives, cause us problems, and make us waste our potential. They arise easily when we think only of the happiness of this life. Reflecting on impermanence and death enlarges our perspective and helps us set our priorities wisely. This, in turn, enables us to turn our attention away from the eight worldly concerns to more important activities, such as cultivating compassion and wisdom.

The Nine-Point Death Meditation

> Like cattle intended for slaughter,
> Death is common to all.
> Moreover when you see others die
> Why do you not fear the Lord of Death?
> Aryadeva, *The Four Hundred*

Considering the mortality of ourselves and others helps us clarify our priorities so that we make our life truly worthwhile and meaningful. Thinking of your own life, consider:

1. Death is inevitable, definite. There is no way to avoid dying. Contemplate:
   - Nothing can prevent our eventually dying. Everyone who is born must die, no matter who we are. Reflect that you and everyone you know and care for will die one day.
   - Our lifespan can't be extended when it is time for us to die. With each passing moment we approach death. We cannot turn the clock back or escape from death.
   - We will die even if we have not had time to practice Dharma.

Conclusion: You must practice the Dharma, that is, you must transform your mind.

2. The time of death is uncertain. We don't know when we'll die. Contemplate:
- In general there is no certainty of lifespan in our world. People die at all ages. There is no guarantee we will live long. Reflect on the people you know who have died. How old were they? What were they doing when they died? Did they expect to die that day?
- There are more opportunities for death and less for remaining alive. It takes great effort to stay alive and very little to die. Protecting our body by feeding, clothing, and sheltering it requires a lot of energy. Dying, on the other hand, requires little effort.
- Our body is extremely fragile. Small things—viruses, bacteria, or pieces of metal—can harm it and cause death.

Conclusion: You must practice Dharma continually, beginning now.

3. Nothing else can help at the time of death except the Dharma. Contemplate:
- Wealth is of no help. Our material possessions can't come with us after death. We spend our lives working hard to accumulate and protect our things. At the time of death, the karma we created doing this comes with us, while we leave the money and possessions behind.
- Friends and relatives are of no help. They remain here while we go on to our next life. However, the karmic seeds of the actions we did in relation to these people come with us into the next life.
- Not even our body is of any help. It is cremated or buried and is of no use to anyone. The karma we created in beautifying, pampering, and seeking pleasure for this body, however, will influence our future experiences.

Conclusion: You must practice the Dharma purely. You may have spent your entire life accumulating and taking care of your wealth, body, friends, and relatives, but at the time of death, you must separate from them without choice. What, then, is the use of chasing after these things while you're alive and creating negative karma to get them? Since your karma comes with you and only your spiritual development aids you at death, isn't it more worthwhile to pay attention to these? Knowing this, what is a healthy and balanced attitude to have towards material possessions, friends and relatives, and your body?

IMAGINING OUR DEATH

The rich and poor alike shall feel (Death's) touch,
The fool and sage as well shall feel it too;
But while the fool lies stricken by his folly,
No sage will ever tremble at the touch.
Ratthapala Sutta

1. Imagine a circumstance in which you are dying. Where you are? How are you dying? How are your friends and family reacting? How do you feel about dying? What is happening in your mind?
2. Ask yourself:
   - Given that I will die one day, what is important in my life?
   - What do I feel good about having done?
   - What do I regret?
   - What do I want to do and to avoid doing while I'm alive?
   - What can I do to prepare for death?
   - What are my priorities in life?

Conclusion: Feel the importance of making your life meaningful. Make specific conclusions about what you want to do and to avoid doing from now on.

Reflecting on our transient nature and mortality makes us concerned with preparing for death and for our future rebirths. To do this, we need guides on the path and thus turn to the Buddhas, Dharma, and Sangha for refuge.

REFUGE: ITS MEANING, CAUSES, AND OBJECTS

> The Blessed One has made the Dharma clear in many ways, as though he were turning upright what had been overthrown, revealing what was hidden, showing the way to one who was lost, or holding up a lamp in the dark for those with eyesight to see forms. Venerable sir, I go to the Blessed One for refuge and to the Dharma and to the Sangha of monastics. Let the Blessed one remember me as a lay follower who has gone to him for refuge for life.
>
> *Upali Sutta, Majjima Nikaya*

1. Refuge means to entrust our spiritual guidance to the Three Jewels: the Buddhas, the Dharma, and the Sangha. Taking refuge opens our heart so that they can teach us and guide us along the path to freedom. Contemplate the effect that taking refuge in the Three Jewels could have on your life and lives.
2. To deepen your refuge, cultivate its causes:
   - Considering what your future would be like if you continued to live on "automatic," be aware of the possibility of experiencing suffering in the future.
   - Thinking about the qualities of the Three Jewels and how they can steer you away from potential suffering and its causes, develop confidence in their ability to guide you.
   - Remembering that others are in the same situation as you, let your compassion for them arise so that you seek a means to progress spiritually for their sake as well as your own.
3. To enrich your faith and confidence in the Three Jewels as objects of refuge, develop a general idea of their qualities:
   - The Buddhas are those who have eliminated all defilements and developed all good qualities completely.
   - The Dharma is the cessations of all unsatisfactory conditions and their causes, and the paths leading to those cessations.
   - The Sangha are those who have direct perception of reality.

Conclusion: With a sense of caution regarding suffering and with confidence in the ability of the Three Jewels, from your heart turn to the Three Jewels for guidance.

REFUGE: AN ANALOGY AND THE QUALITIES OF THE THREE JEWELS

Bound himself in the jail of cyclic existence,
What worldly god can give you protection?
Therefore when you seek refuge, take refuge in
The Three Jewels which will not betray you—
This is the practice of bodhisattvas.
Gyelsay Togmay Sangpo, *The Thirty-seven Practices of Bodhisattvas*

1. Contemplate the analogy of a sick person seeking a cure to his illness. Beings trapped in cyclic existence are like sick people. We turn to the Buddha, who is like a doctor, to diagnose our illness and prescribe a cure. The Dharma is the medicine we must take and the Sangha are the nurses who help us take it. In this way, we can be liberated from misery.

2. To enhance your faith and confidence, consider why the Buddhas are suitable guides on the path:
   - They are free from the extremes of cyclic existence and self-complacent peace.
   - They have skillful and effective means to free others from all fear.
   - They have equal compassion for all, regardless of whether we have faith in them or not.
   - They fulfill the aims of all beings whether or not those beings have helped them.

Conclusion: From your heart, make a determination to follow these reliable guides and to put into practice their guidance.

Having entrusted our spiritual guidance to the Three Jewels, we want to follow their counsel. The first advice they give us is to stop harming others and ourselves. We do this by observing actions (karma) and their effects.

THE LAW OF KARMA AND ITS EFFECTS

These beings who engaged in misconduct of body, speech, and mind, who reviled the noble ones, held wrong view, and undertook actions based on wrong view, with the breakup of the body, after death, have been reborn in a state of misery, in a bad destination, in the nether world, in hell; but these beings who engaged in good conduct of body, speech, and mind, who did not revile the noble ones, who held right view, and undertook action based on right view, with the breakup of the body, after death, have been reborn in a good destination, in a heavenly world.

The Book of Causation, Samyutta Nikaya

Karma is intentional action. Such actions leave latencies on our mindstream that influence what we will experience in the future. Karma has four general aspects. Relate each of these to events in your life:

1. Karma is definite. Happiness always comes from constructive actions and pain from destructive ones. Therefore it is to our advantage to create the former and abandon the latter.
2. Karma is expandable. A small cause can lead to a large result. Thus we should take care to abandon even small negativities, and to do even small constructive actions.
3. If the cause hasn't been created, the result won't be experienced. If we don't act destructively, we will not experience hardships and obstacles; if we don't create the cause for realizations of the path, we will not gain them.
4. Karmic latencies do not get lost; we will experience their results. However, negative latencies can be purified by the four opponent powers and positive latencies can be impaired by our getting angry or generating distorted views.

Conclusion: Determine to observe your motivations and actions so you create the causes of happiness and avoid the causes of suffering.

The Ten Nonvirtues

> His action marks the fool, his action marks the wise person, O monastics. Wisdom shines forth in behavior. By three things the fool can be known: by bad conduct of body, speech, and mind. By three things the wise person can be known: by good conduct of body, speech, and mind.
>
> Buddha, "The Fool and the Wise Person," *Anguttara Nikaya*

Doing a life review to take stock of our harmful and beneficial actions enables us to purify the former and develop a strong intention to live wisely and compassionately in the future. To do this, reflect on which destructive actions you have done. Understand how you got involved in them, as well as their immediate and long-term results. The ten nonvirtues are:

1. killing: taking the life of any sentient being, including animals
2. stealing: taking what has not been given to you. This includes not paying fees or taxes that you owe, using supplies at your workplace for your own personal use without permission, and not returning things you have borrowed.
3. unwise sexual behavior: adultery and carelessly using sexuality in a way that harms others physically or emotionally
4. lying: deliberately deceiving others
5. divisive speech: causing others to be disharmonious or preventing them from reconciling
6. harsh words: insulting, abusing, ridiculing, teasing, or deliberately hurting another's feelings
7. idle talk: talking about unimportant topics for no particular purpose
8. coveting: desiring possessions that belong to others and planning how to obtain them

9. maliciousness: planning to hurt others or to take revenge on them
10. distorted views: strongly holding to cynical views that deny the existence of important things, such as the possibility of becoming enlightened, rebirth, karma, and the Three Jewels

Conclusion: Experience a sense of relief because you have been honest with yourself about the past. Remember you can purify the latencies of these mistaken actions. Resolve to direct your energy in constructive directions and to avoid acting in ways that harm yourself and others.

THE RESULTS OF KARMA

> It is, monastics, as with seeds that are undamaged, not rotten, unspoiled by wind and sun, capable of sprouting and well embedded in a good field, sown in well-prepared soil: if there is plenty of rain, these seeds will grow, shoot up, and develop abundantly. Similarly, monastics, whatever action is done out of attachment, hatred, or confusion will ripen wherever the individual is reborn; and wherever the action ripens, there the individual experiences the fruit, be it in this life, or the next life, or in subsequent future lives.
>
> Buddha, "Causes of Action," *Anguttara Nikaya*

Each complete action—that is, one with preparation, actual action, and completion—brings four results. Contemplating the relationship between specific actions and their effects helps us to understand the causes of our present experiences and the future results of our present actions. This, in turn, enables us to take responsibility for our happiness by avoiding destructive actions, purifying those already done, and acting constructively. For each of the ten virtues and nonvirtues, contemplate their:

1. ripening result. In general, this refers to the body and mind we take in our future lives. All destructive actions result in unfortunate rebirths. All constructive actions result in happy rebirths.
2. result corresponding to the cause:
   - in terms of our experience. We experience things similar to what we have caused others to experience. For example, if we criticize others, we will receive unfair criticism.
   - in terms of our actions. Each action causes us to form habitual behavior patterns. For example, frequent lying develops in us the habit of lying.
3. environmental result. We live in a pleasant or unpleasant place. For example, divisive, disharmonious speech brings rebirth in an inhospitable environment with severe storms.

Conclusion: Not wanting to experience the painful or unpleasant results of your harmful deeds, resolve to purify them through applying the four opponent powers.

THE FOUR OPPONENT POWERS FOR PURIFICATION

> Maitreya, if bodhisattvas, the great heroes, possess these four teachings, then they will overcome any negativities that they have committed and accumulated. What are the four? They are the power of eradication, the power of applying remedies, the power of turning away from faults, and the power of the foundation.
>
> *The Sutra Giving the Four Teachings*

Doing the four opponent powers repeatedly can purify the karmic latencies of our destructive actions and relieve the psychological heaviness of guilt. Contemplate:

1. the power of regret. Visualize the Buddhas and bodhisattvas in front of you and generate regret (not guilt!) for your negative actions and motivations by honestly admitting them. Feel that the Buddhas and bodhisattvas witness your unburden-

ing these things and look at you with complete acceptance and compassion.

2. the power of the foundation. Repair the relationship with those whom you have harmed. In the case of holy beings, reaffirm your refuge in them. In the case of ordinary beings, generate a positive attitude towards them and the altruistic intention to benefit them in the future. If it is possible to do so, apologize to those you have harmed. When it is not possible, focus on wishing them well.

3. the power of turning away from faults. Make a determination not to do the actions again in the future. For those actions you cannot honestly say you will never do again, make a determination to abandon them for a specific amount of time that is reasonable for you.

4. the power of remedial behavior. This may be community service, spiritual practice, prostrations, making offerings, visualizing light and nectar flowing from the Buddhas into you while you recite mantra, meditating on bodhicitta or emptiness, and so forth.

Conclusion: Feel you have purified all negative karmic latencies and released all guilt. Feel psychologically and spiritually cleansed so you can go on with your life with a fresh and positive attitude.

CONSTRUCTIVE ACTIONS

> Likewise when karma and its effects are thoroughly analyzed,
> Though they do not exist as intrinsically one or many,
> Like apparitions they effect the risings and cessations of phenomena.
> Seemingly real, one experiences joy and pain of every kind.
> So within this mere appearance I'll follow the norms of ethical conduct.
> Dharmarakshita, *The Wheel-Weapon Training of Mind*

It is equally important to be aware of our constructive actions, our motivations for doing them, and their results. For each type of positive action mentioned below:

- Think of specific examples of the times you have engaged in it.
- What was your motivation?
- How did you do the action?
- What were the short- and long-term results?
- How can you protect your tendencies to act constructively? How can you increase your positive actions?

Constructive actions include:

1. being in a situation in which we could act negatively but choosing not to do so
2. doing the ten virtues, which are the opposite of the ten nonvirtues. For example, saving life is the opposite of killing, protecting and respecting others' possessions is the opposite of stealing, and so forth.
3. cultivating the six far-reaching practices: generosity, ethical discipline, patience, joyous effort, concentration, and wisdom

Conclusion: Rejoice at the positive deeds you have done and encourage yourself to act in beneficial ways in the future.

By gaining a firm understanding of the meditations in common with the initial level practitioner, we begin to change our attitudes and behavior. As a result, we are happier and get along better with others. In addition, we create the causes for a peaceful death and a good rebirth.

THE PATH IN COMMON WITH THE MIDDLE LEVEL PRACTITIONER

As we go deeper into Dharma practice, we see that while preparing for our future lives is important, it does not free us from cyclic existence altogether. For this reason, we contemplate the various disadvantages and sufferings of cyclic existence and its causes in order to generate the determination to be free from it and to attain liberation (nirvana).

THE EIGHT SUFFERINGS OF HUMAN BEINGS

> In worldly existence there is never
> Rebirth of one's own free will.
> Being under others' control,
> Who with intelligence would be fearless?
> > Aryadeva, *The Four Hundred*

To get a better sense of the unsatisfactory conditions of our present situation, consider the difficulties we experience as human beings:

1. birth. Is being in the womb and then going through the birth process comfortable, or is it confusing?
2. aging. Imagine yourself as an old person. How do you feel about the inevitable decline of your physical and mental abilities?
3. sickness. How does it feel to get sick without choice or control?
4. death. Is death something you look forward to?
5. being separated from what we like. Think about the suffering involved when this has happened to you.
6. meeting with what we don't like. How does it feel when problems come even though you don't want them?

7. not obtaining the things we like even though we try so hard to get them. Think of examples of this from your life. Do you like this situation?
8. having a body and mind under the control of afflictions and karma. Reflect that the very nature of your present body and mind is unsatisfactory because you have very little control over them. For example, you cannot stop your body from aging and dying, and it is difficult to deal with strong negative emotions and to concentrate your mind during meditation.

Conclusion: Develop the determination to free yourself from cyclic existence and to practice the path to do so. While this aspiration is sometimes translated as "renunciation" (of suffering and its causes), it actually is having compassion for ourselves and wanting ourselves to have lasting Dharma happiness.

THE SIX DIFFICULTIES OF CYCLIC EXISTENCE

> When there is no end at all
> To this ocean of suffering,
> Why are you childish people
> Not afraid of drowning in it?
> Aryadeva, *The Four Hundred*

To develop a strong determination to be free from cyclic existence and to attain liberation, contemplate the unsatisfactory conditions of cyclic existence by contemplating many examples from your life:

1. There is no certainty, security, or stability in our lives. For example, we try to be financially secure or secure in our relationships, but this constantly eludes us.
2. We are never satisfied with what we have, what we do, or who we are. We always want more and better. Dissatisfaction often pervades our lives.

3. We die repeatedly, in one life after another.
4. We take rebirth repeatedly, without choice.
5. We change status—from exalted to humble—repeatedly. Sometimes we are rich, other times poor. Sometimes we are respected, other times people are condescending towards us.
6. We undergo suffering alone. No one else can experience it for us.

Conclusion: Wanting to be free from cyclic existence, generate the determination to attain liberation (nirvana).

THE CAUSES OF CYCLIC EXISTENCE

> A mental affliction is defined as a phenomenon that, when it arises, is disturbing in character and that, through arising, disturbs the mindstream.
> Asanga, *Compendium of Knowledge*

Our unsatisfactory experience of being in cyclic existence has causes—the afflictions (disturbing attitudes and negative emotions) in our mind. Think of examples of the following mental afflictions in your life:

1. attachment: exaggerating or projecting good qualities and then clinging to the object
2. anger: exaggerating or projecting bad qualities and then wishing to harm or get away from what makes us miserable
3. pride: an inflated sense of self that makes us feel we are either the best or the worst of all
4. ignorance: a lack of clarity regarding the nature of things and active misconceptions about the nature of reality and about karma and its effects
5. deluded doubt: doubt tending towards incorrect conclusions
6. distorted views: wrong conceptions
   - view of the transitory collection: the conception of an inherent "I" or "mine" (grasping at the self as inherently existent)

- view holding to an extreme: absolutism (grasping at inherent existence; eternalism) or nihilism (believing that nothing at all exists)
- distorted views: denying the existence of cause and effect, rebirth, enlightenment, and the Three Jewels
- holding distorted views as supreme: thinking the above are the best views
- holding bad ethics and modes of conduct as supreme: thinking that unethical actions are ethical and that incorrect practices are the path to liberation

For each one of the mental afflictions, consider:

- How does it cause you problems now by unrealistically interpreting events in your life?
- How does it bring about future unhappiness by making you create the cause, negative karma?
- What antidotes can you apply when it arises in your mind?
- Which one of these is the strongest for you? Have an especially strong aspiration to be aware of and to counteract this one.

Conclusion: Seeing the damage these mental afflictions cause in your life, develop the determination to be aware of their arising and to learn and practice the antidotes to them.

FACTORS THAT STIMULATE THE ARISING OF MENTAL AFFLICTIONS

In brief, whatever you are doing,
Ask yourself, "What's the state of my mind?"
With constant mindfulness and mental alertness
Accomplish others' good—
This is the practice of bodhisattvas.
Gyelsay Togmay Sangpo, *The Thirty-seven Practices of Bodhisattvas*

Contemplating examples from your life, understand how the following factors stimulate the arising of negative emotions and misconceptions:

1. the latencies of the afflictions. Do you have the seed or potential to generate disturbing attitudes and negative emotions even though they may not be manifest in your mind now?
2. contact with the object. What objects, people, or situations trigger the arising of disturbing attitudes and negative emotions in you? How can you be more aware when you encounter these people, situations, or objects?
3. detrimental influences such as bad friends. How much does peer pressure or what other people think of you influence your behavior? Are you strongly influenced by friends or relatives who act unethically or who distract you from the spiritual path?
4. verbal stimuli—media, books, TV, Internet, radio, magazines, etc. How much do the media shape what you believe and your self-image? How much time do you spend listening to, watching, or reading the media? How can you have a healthy and reasonable relationship with the media so that they don't control your life and your thoughts?
5. habitual ways of thinking, habitual emotions. What emotional habits or patterns do you have?
6. inappropriate attention. Do you pay attention to negative aspects of situations? Do you have many biases? Are you quick to jump to conclusions or be judgmental? What steps can you take to remedy these tendencies?

Conclusion: Understanding the disadvantages of the afflictions, determine to abandon them. Think of how you can avoid the factors causing their arising and determine to change your lifestyle accordingly.

The Paths That Cease the Disturbing Attitudes, Negative Emotions, and Karma

Through ethical discipline, concentration, and wisdom,
Achieve nirvana, an undefiled state of peace and restraint:
Ageless, deathless, inexhaustible;
Free from earth, water, fire, wind, sun, and moon.
> Nagarjuna, *Friendly Letter*

The Three Higher Trainings—in ethical conduct, meditative stabilization, and wisdom—are the paths to cease our unsatisfactory conditions and to attain a state of lasting peace and happiness. For each of the higher trainings, reflect:

1. What advantages accrue now and in the future by practicing this training?
2. How can you implement this training in your daily life? Have some specific ideas and make a firm determination to do this.
3. How does each higher training build upon the previous one? Why are they practiced in this order?

Conclusion: Understanding how the Three Higher Trainings will lead you to liberation from cyclic existence, make a determination to practice them and actualize them with joyous effort.

THE PATH OF THE ADVANCED PRACTITIONER

Although we practice the paths in common with the initial and middle level practition-ers, we do not stop with the attainment of their objectives, of upper rebirth and libera-tion, respectively. Rather, seeing that all sentient beings, who have all been kind to us in our many lives, are in the same situation, we work to generate bodhicitta—the altruis-tic intention to attain enlightenment in order to benefit all sentient beings most effec-tively. This is the motivation of the higher level practitioner. The foundation for bodhicitta is equanimity, an attitude that is free from bias, aversion, clinging attach-ment, and apathy towards others and that cares about them equally.

> When people see that joy and unhappiness are like a dream
> And that beings degenerate due to the faults of delusion,
> Why would they strive for their own welfare,
> Forsaking delight in the excellent deeds of altruism?
> Aryashura, *Compendium of the Perfections*

EQUANIMITY

> From living beings' viewpoint, all equally want happiness and do not want suffering. Therefore, it is inappropriate to hold some close and to help them, while keeping others at a distance and harming or not helping them ... From my viewpoint, if I have continuously been reborn since begin-ningless time, all beings have been my friends hundreds of times. To whom should I be attached? To whom should I be hostile?
> Je Tsongkhapa, *The Great Treatise on the Stages of the Path*

1. Visualize three people: a friend, a person you have difficulty with, and a stranger. Ask yourself, "Why do I feel attachment for my friend?" Listen to the reasons your mind gives. Then ask, "Why do I have aversion toward the difficult person?" and do the same. Finally, explore, "Why am I apathetic toward the stranger?"

2. What word do you keep hearing in all these reasons? On what basis does your mind consider someone good, bad, or neutral? On what basis do you discriminate someone as a friend, disagreeable person, or stranger? Is it realistic to judge others based on how they relate to "ME"? Are others really good, bad, or neutral from their own side, or is it your mind that categorizes them as such? How would others appear to you if you stopped discriminating them as friend, enemy, or stranger based on your own self-centered opinions, needs, and wants?

3. The relationships of friend, difficult person, and stranger change constantly. One person can be all three within a short period of time. If someone insults you yesterday and praises you today and another person praised you yesterday and insults you today, which one is your friend? Which one is the difficult person?

Conclusion: Acknowledging that your attitudes create the seemingly solid relationships of friend, difficult person, and stranger, let go of the attachment, anger, and apathy you feel towards others. Let yourself feel an openhearted concern for all beings.

Before we can feel genuine love and compassion for others, we must see them as lovable. Seeing them as our parents or kind caregivers and remembering their kindness to us, both when they are our parents or caregivers and when they are not, enables us to have a positive view of them.

ALL SENTIENT BEINGS HAVE BEEN OUR PARENTS, THEIR KINDNESS, AND REPAYING THEIR KINDNESS

> When your mothers, who have loved you since time without beginning,
> Are suffering, what use is your own happiness?
> Therefore to free limitless living beings
> Develop the altruistic intention—
> This is the practice of bodhisattvas.
> Gyelsay Togmay Sangpo, *The Thirty-seven Practices of Bodhisattvas*

1. Since beginningless time, we have taken one rebirth after the other, in many types of bodies in all the realms of cyclic existence. As human beings, animals, and hungry ghosts, we have had mothers who have given birth to us. Since our previous lives are infinite, all sentient beings, at one time or another, have been our mothers and fathers. Seeing that others are not just who they appear to be today, try to get a sense of your beginningless connection to them.

2. When they have been our parents, each sentient being has been kind to us, loving us as parents love their children. As an example of the kindness of parents, remember the kindness that the parents of your present life have shown you. If it is easier for you to think of the kindness of another relative, friend, or caregiver, do that. As you consider each example of kindness, let yourself feel gratitude towards the person. If, in the process of recalling childhood events, painful memories arise, remember that your parents are ordinary sentient beings who did their best, given their abilities and the situations in which they found themselves. For example:

   - Our mother happily bore the discomfort of being pregnant and giving birth to us.
   - Our parents took care of us when we were infants and toddlers and could not care for ourselves. They protected us from danger and got up in the middle of the night to feed us even when they were tired.
   - They taught us how to speak and how to take care of our basic needs. We learned so many small, yet essential, skills from them, such as how to tie our shoes, how to cook, how to clean up after ourselves, and so forth.
   - As children we predominantly thought of ourselves only, and our parents had to teach us manners, social skills, and how to get along with others.
   - They gave us an education.
   - They worked hard to get the finances to give us a place to live, toys, and other enjoyments.

3. Since all sentient beings have been our parents, they too have shown us similar kindness again and again.

4. Remembering their kindness and knowing that you have been the recipient of

so much kindness from them throughout your beginningless lifetimes, let a wish to repay their kindness arise naturally in your heart. Let your mind rest in these feelings.

THE KINDNESS OF OTHERS

> Meditate on the great kindness of all.
> Geshe Chekawa, *Seven-Point Thought Transformation*

To develop an awareness of your interconnectedness with all others and the sense of being the recipient of much kindness from them, contemplate:

1. the help we've received from friends. This includes the support, encouragement, gifts, practical help, and so forth that we've received from them. Do not think of the friends in a way that increases attachment to them. Instead, recognize their help as acts of human kindness and feel grateful.
2. the benefit we've received from parents, relatives, and teachers. Reflect on the care they gave us when we were young, protecting us from danger and giving us an education. The fact that we can speak comes from the efforts of those who cared for us when we were young, including our teachers. All talents, abilities, and skills we have now are due to the people who taught and trained us. Even when we didn't want to learn and were unruly, they continued trying to help us learn.
3. the help we've received from strangers. The buildings we use, clothes we wear, food we eat, and roads we drive on were all made by people we don't know. Without their effort—the contribution they make to society by whatever work they do—we wouldn't be able to survive.
4. the benefit we've received from people we don't get along with and from people who have harmed us. These people show us what we need to work on and point out our weaknesses so that we can improve. They give us the chance to develop patience, tolerance, and compassion, qualities that are essential for progressing along the path.

Conclusion: Recognize that you've received incalculable benefit and help from others throughout your lifetime. Let yourself experience the care, kindness, and love that others have shown you. Let a sense of gratitude arise and generate the wish to be kind to them in return.

EQUALIZING SELF AND OTHERS

By becoming accustomed to the equality of self and other,
The altruistic intention becomes firm.
Self and other are interdependent.
Like this side and the other side of a river, they are false.

The other bank is not in itself "other,"
In relation to someone else it is "this bank."
Similarly "self" does not exist in its own right;
In relation to someone else, it is "other."
                    Shantideva, *Compendium of Trainings*

To feel that all sentient beings—friends, strangers, difficult people, self, and others—are equally worthy of respect and help and are equally valuable, contemplate the following nine points:

1. All beings want to be happy and to avoid pain as intensely as we do. Try to look at each individual you see with this thought in mind.
2. Ten patients may suffer from different illness, but all want to be cured. Similarly, sentient beings have different problems, but all equally want to be free from them. There is no reason for us to be partial, thinking some beings are more important than others.
3. Ten beggars may need different things, but all want to be happy. Similarly, each sentient being may want different things, but all want to be happy. It would be unfair for us to have a discriminatory attitude, helping some and ignoring others.

Conclusion: All beings, including yourself, equally want to be happy and avoid suffering. Think that you must work to eliminate the suffering of all equally and help all equally. Although you cannot do this externally, you can hold this attitude internally.

4. All beings have helped us so much. The mere fact that we've been able to stay alive since birth is due to the efforts of others. Reflect on the help you have received throughout your lifetime.
5. Even if some people have harmed us, the benefit we receive from them far outweighs this.
6. Holding grudges against those who have harmed us is counterproductive.

Conclusion: Let the wish to help others arise in your heart. Let go of any wish for revenge or retaliation for past harms.

7. The relationships of friend, disagreeable person, and stranger aren't fixed; they change easily.
8. The Buddha sees no inherent friend, difficult person, or stranger, so do they exist?
9. Self and other is not an inherent distinction between people. It is purely nominal and dependent, like this side of the valley and the other side.

Conclusion: There is no difference on a conventional or an ultimate level between yourself and others. Feeling this in your heart, give up any attitude of partiality that favors yourself or your dear ones and open your heart to respect and cherish all beings. Although you may not act the same with everyone—you must still accord with certain social roles and consider others' abilities—in your heart you can still wish them well equally.

Having an equal attitude to all beings and seeing them as lovable and worthy of happiness, we now focus on uprooting the principal impediment to altruism, our self-centered attitude. In addition, we cultivate the mind that cherishes others and, based on that, generate love and compassion.

THE DISADVANTAGES OF SELF-CENTEREDNESS

> Though wishing greatly for happiness is great, I do not seek its conditions, the merits;
> Though having little endurance for hardship, I am rife with greed, the dark craving–
> Dance and trample on the head of this betrayer, false conception.
> Mortally strike at the heart of this butcher, the enemy, the self(-centeredness).
> Dharmarakshita, *The Wheel-Weapon Training of Mind*

We are not our self-centered attitude, which is an attitude clouding the pure nature of our minds. We and our selfishness are not one and the same, and thus self-preoccupation can be eliminated from our mindstreams. By reflecting on experiences in your life, you can see how your self-centered attitude has caused you harm and thus wish to overcome it. Our self-centeredness:

1. makes us act in ways that harm others
2. causes us to act in ways we later regret and is the root of self-hatred
3. makes us overly sensitive and easily offended
4. is the basis for all fear
5. breeds dissatisfaction. It's impossible to satisfy the bottomless pit of our desires.
6. underlies all conflict between individuals, groups, and nations
7. motivates us to do harmful actions in a confused attempt to be happy. We thus create negative karma, bringing undesirable situations upon ourselves in the future. Our current problems are results of our past selfish actions.
8. impedes our spiritual progress and prevents enlightenment

Conclusion: See self-centeredness as your real enemy and determine not to let yourself fall under its sway.

The Advantages of Cherishing Others

> Whatever worldly joy there is
> Arises from wishing for others' happiness.
> Whatever worldly suffering there is
> Arises from wishing for your own happiness.
>
> What need is there to say more?
> Look at the difference between these two:
> Ordinary persons act for their own welfare;
> The Sage acts for others' welfare.
> > Shantideva, *A Guide to the Bodhisattva's Way of Life*

Thinking of examples from your own and others' lives, reflect on the benefit of cherishing others that accrues to both yourself and others:

1. Other sentient beings are happy.
2. Our lives become meaningful.
3. We overcome our self-centered ways that make us so miserable.
4. We can be happy anywhere, anytime, no matter whom we are with.
5. Our relationships flourish.
6. We feel joyful and at peace with ourselves.
7. We will not suffer from fear, anxiety, or worry.
8. Harmony in society increases.
9. We create great positive potential, thus creating the cause for good rebirths and making it easier for us to gain realizations of the path.
10. Cherishing others is the root of all happiness of self and others, now and in the future.

Conclusion: Resolve to care for others with genuine affection. Recognize the difference between sincerely caring for others and caring for them out of guilt, obligation, fear, or codependency.

LOVE

A noble disciple—devoid of covetousness, devoid of ill will, unconfused, clearly comprehending, ever mindful—dwells pervading one quarter with a mind imbued with loving-kindness, likewise the second quarter, the third, and the fourth. Thus above, below, across, and everywhere, and to all as to himself, he dwells pervading the entire world with a mind imbued with loving-kindness, vast, exalted, measureless, without hostility, and without ill will.

"The Four Boundless States," *Anguttara Nikaya*

Love is the wish for sentient beings, including yourself, to have happiness and its causes.

1. Reflect: What is happiness? Think of the short-term benefits of temporal happiness (the happiness experienced in cyclic existence) such as that received from having wealth, friends, reputation, health, good rebirths, and so forth. Think of the long-term benefits of happiness received from practicing the Dharma: mental happiness and peace of mind, liberation, and enlightenment.
2. Begin by wishing yourself to have these two types of happiness, not in a selfish way, but because you respect and care for yourself as one of many sentient beings. Imagine yourself being happy in these ways.
3. Wish that your friends and dear ones have these two kinds of happiness. Think, feel, and imagine, "May my friends and all those who have been kind to me have happiness and its causes. May they be free of suffering, confusion, and fear. May they have calm, peaceful, and fulfilled hearts. May they be liberated from all the miseries of cyclic existence. May they attain the bliss of enlightenment." For this and each of the following groups of people, think of specific individuals and generate these thoughts and feelings towards them. Then generalize to the entire group.
4. Generate the same loving feeling towards those who are strangers.

5. Spread your love to those who have harmed you or with whom you don't get along. Recognize that they do what you find objectionable because they are experiencing pain or confusion. How wonderful it would be if they were free from those.

6. Generate love for all sentient beings. Think of those beings in all realms of existence—hell beings, hungry ghosts, animals, human beings, demi-gods, and gods. Generate love towards arhats and bodhisattvas as well.

Conclusion: Let your mind rest single-pointedly in this feeling of love for all beings.

COMPASSION

> Thus as I take on myself all the negative deeds of others
> Committed through their three doors throughout all three times,
> Like a peacock that possesses colorful feathers because of poison,
> May the afflictions transform into factors of enlightenment.
> Dharmarakshita, *The Wheel-Weapon Training of Mind*

Compassion is the wish for sentient beings, including yourself, to be free from suffering and its causes.

1. Remember a time when your mind was filled with fear and aggression. Imagine it becoming your entire reality, so that it manifests as your body and environment—the hell realms. Think that others are experiencing that right now and develop compassion for them, wishing them to be free from that suffering.

2. Remember a time when craving and dissatisfaction overwhelmed your mind such that you ran everywhere searching for happiness but, unable to enjoy what you had, wanted more. Imagine it becoming so intense that it becomes your body and environment—the hungry ghost realm. Think that others are experiencing that right now and develop compassion for them, wishing them to be free from that suffering.

3. Remember a time when your mind was clouded with deep ignorance and confusion such that you could not think clearly or use your wisdom. Imagine it becoming so intense that it becomes your body and environment—the animal realm. Think that others are experiencing that right now and develop compassion for them, wishing them to be free from that suffering.

4. Reflect on the eight sufferings of human beings that you contemplated previously. Think that others are experiencing those right now and develop compassion for them, wishing them to be free from that suffering.

5. Remember a time when your mind was so saturated with pleasure that you became completely self-absorbed. Distracted by the pleasure, you could not focus your mind on anything meaningful and could not open your heart to others. Imagine it becoming so intense that it becomes your body and environment—the celestial realms. Think that others are experiencing that right now and develop compassion for them, wishing them to be free from that suffering.

Conclusion: Rest your mind single-pointedly in feeling compassion for all beings.

EXCHANGING SELF AND OTHERS

> When fear and suffering are equally abhorrent to others and myself, then
> what is so special about me that I protect myself but not others?
> Shantideva, *A Guide to the Bodhisattva's Way of Life*

Exchanging self and others does not mean "I become you and you become me." It means changing who is important and cherished from self to others. To do this, reflect:

1. Suffering is suffering. No matter whose it is—mine or others'—it is to be removed.

2. Although we think of our body as "mine," in fact it is not. Our genes came from the sperm and egg of our parents, and the food that made the fertilized egg grow into an adult came from other beings. It is only due to the force of familiarity that we grasp this body as "mine," and therefore as important and worthy of com-

fort and happiness. Similarly, through familiarity, we can come to consider others' happiness as important and worthy as we now consider our own.

Conclusion: Exchange ourselves and others, wishing that others be happy in the same way that you now wish yourself to be happy.

Taking and Giving

> All suffering comes from the wish for your own happiness.
> Perfect Buddhas are born from the thought to help others.
> Therefore exchange your own happiness
> For the suffering of others—
> This is the practice of bodhisattvas.
>> Gyelsay Togmay Sangpo, *The Thirty-seven Practices of Bodhisattvas*

In our current self-centered confusion, whenever we are able to, we take any goodness and happiness for ourselves and give any difficulties and discomfort to others. Seeing the disadvantages of self-preoccupation and the advantages of cherishing others, and exchanging your wish for happiness from self to others, now cultivate strong compassion wishing to take their problems and give them your happiness.

1. Imagine in front of you a person or group of people who are experiencing difficulties in some way. Think, "How wonderful it would be if I could experience those problems instead of them." Imagine taking on their problems and confusion by inhaling them in the form of black smoke.
2. The smoke turns into a thunderbolt or bomb, which completely obliterates the black lump of selfishness and ignorance at your heart.
3. Feel the open space, the lack of wrong conception about self and others. Rest in that spaciousness.
4. In this space, imagine a white light—the nature of your love—that radiates to all beings. Imagine you multiply and transform your body, possessions, and positive

potential into whatever others need. With delight, give them to those people.

5. Imagine them being satisfied and happy. Think that they have all the circumstances conducive to attaining enlightenment. Rejoice that you've been able to bring this about.

At the beginning, do this meditation slowly and use specific people or groups. As you become more familiar with it, enlarge the group with whom you do the taking and giving meditation, until it becomes all sentient beings of the six realms.

Conclusion: Feel you are strong enough to take on others' misery and give them your happiness. Be glad that you can imagine doing this and pray to be able to actually do this.

THE GREAT RESOLVE AND THE ALTRUISTIC INTENTION (BODHICITTA)

> Upon mounting the chariot of bodhicitta
> Which carries away all despondency and weariness,
> What sensible person would despair
> At progressing in this way from joy to joy?
> Shantideva, *A Guide to the Bodhisattva's Way of Life*

1. To generate the great resolve, make a strong determination to take the responsibility yourself to liberate all sentient beings from cyclic existence and bring them to Buddhahood. That is, pledge to make the goals of your love and compassion a reality.

2. To generate the altruistic intention, contemplate the fact that you will be best equipped to work for the benefit of others when your own compassion, wisdom, and skill are fully developed. Then aspire to attain full enlightenment—the state in which all defilements are totally eradicated and all good qualities are fully developed—in order to be able to best benefit others.

Conclusion: Feel joyful that you have generated bodhicitta (the altruistic intention).

Once we have generated bodhicitta, we must engage in the six far-reaching practices (the six paramitas or six perfections) to complete the accumulation of positive potential and the accumulation of wisdom that are needed to attain enlightenment. These six practices—generosity, ethical conduct, patience, joyous effort, meditative stabilization, and wisdom—become far-reaching practices when they are motivated and held by the altruistic intention. They are purified and realized when they are held by the wisdom realizing the emptiness of the circle of three: the agent, action, and object. Therefore, try to practice each far-reaching attitude with the motivation of bodhicitta, seal it with an understanding of emptiness, and dedicate the positive potential for the enlightenment of ourselves and all others.

Each far-reaching practice should be practiced together with the others. For example, the ethical conduct of generosity is not to harm others while giving. The patience of generosity is not to become angry if those we give to are unappreciative or rude. The joyous effort of generosity is to take delight in giving. The concentration of generosity is to maintain an altruistic intention while giving and to give without distraction. The wisdom of generosity is to reflect upon the emptiness of the circle of three. Integrating each far-reaching practice into the others can be understood from this example.

FAR-REACHING GENEROSITY

> For the sake of accomplishing the welfare of all sentient beings, I freely give my body, enjoyments, and all my virtues of the three times.
> Shantideva, *A Guide to the Bodhisattva's Way of Life*

Generosity is the wish to give our body, possessions, and positive potential to others without the wish to receive anything—including appreciation—in return. The three types of generosity are:

1. giving material possessions to those in need, including people you know and don't know, and people you like and don't like
2. giving protection to those in danger: travelers, insects who are drowning in water, children who are fighting, etc.
3. giving wise advice and Dharma teachings to those who need them. This includes helping to calm friends who are angry, saying prayers and mantras aloud so animals nearby can hear them, leading meditations, and teaching the Dharma.

For each of these:

- Think about what you can give.
- Think about to whom you can give and how you can give.
- Cultivate the altruistic intention and then imagine giving to others.

Meditating in this way prepares you to actually be generous in your daily life.

Conclusion: Understanding what, how, and to whom you can give, now rejoice when you have the opportunity to give. Share with others and take delight in being generous.

FAR-REACHING ETHICAL CONDUCT

> Without ethical conduct you can't accomplish your own well-being,
> So wanting to accomplish others' is laughable.
> Therefore without worldly aspirations
> Safeguard your ethical discipline—
> This is the practice of bodhisattvas.
> > Gyelsay Togmay Sangpo, *The Thirty-seven Practices of Bodhisattvas*

Ethical conduct is the wish to abandon harming all others. For each of the following types of ethical conduct, contemplate:

- your motivation for doing it
- the actions involved in doing it

1. abandoning destructive actions, for example, refraining from the ten nonvirtues
2. engaging in constructive actions, for example, joyfully taking opportunities to act constructively
3. benefiting others by:
   - helping the suffering or sick
   - giving counsel and advice to those who are obscured or ignorant of means to help themselves
   - providing help to those who need it to realize their goals
   - protecting those who are afraid, in danger, or about to be killed or injured
   - comforting those who are grieving, whose relative has died, or who have lost their social position
   - helping the poor and needy
   - providing for those who are in need of a place to stay, such as the poor, Dharma practitioners, and travelers
   - helping to reconcile those who quarrel and seek to be in harmony
   - supporting those who wish to practice the Dharma and act constructively
   - stopping those who are acting negatively or are about to do so
   - using clairvoyant powers, if one has them, to prove the validity of the Dharma if all other methods fail or to stop others' negative actions

Conclusion: Feel joyful to practice ethical conduct with altruism and an awareness of emptiness.

FAR-REACHING PATIENCE

> Just as a physician is not upset with
> Someone who rages while possessed by a demon,
> Subduers see disturbing emotions as
> The enemy, not the person who has them.
> Aryadeva, *The Four Hundred*

Anger (or hostility) can arise towards people, objects, or our own suffering (for example, when we are sick or mentally unhappy). It arises due to exaggerating the negative qualities of a person, object, or situation, or by superimposing negative qualities that aren't there. Anger then wants to harm the source of the unhappiness. Anger (hostility) is a generic term that includes being irritated, annoyed, critical, judgmental, self-righteous, belligerent, and hostile.

The Disadvantages of Anger

> The mind does not find peace,
> Nor does it enjoy pleasure and joy,
> Nor does it find sleep or fortitude
> When the thorn of hatred dwells in the heart.
> Shantideva, *A Guide to the Bodhisattva's Way of Life*

By reflecting on your own experiences, examine if anger is destructive or if it is useful.

1. Are you happy when you're angry?
2. Do you see a pattern in the type of situations in which you become angry or the people with whom you get angry? What effect does this pattern have on your life?
3. How do you feel when you're angry? Underneath the anger, is there hurt? Fear? Sadness? Anger often makes us feel powerful when inside we feel powerless. Getting in touch with the feeling behind the anger can help us understand it better.

4. Do you communicate with others effectively when you're angry? Do you aggressively lash out at them? Do you withdraw and not speak?

5. What is the effect of your actions on others? Does your anger bring about the happiness that you desire?

6. Later when you're calm, how do you feel about what you said and did when you were angry? Is there shame, guilt, or loss of self-esteem?

7. How do you appear in others' eyes when you're angry? Does anger promote mutual respect, harmony, and friendship?

Conclusion: Seeing that anger and resentment destroy your own and others' happiness, determine to observe when it arises and to apply the Dharma antidotes to subdue it.

The Antidotes to Anger

> While the enemy of your own anger is unsubdued,
> Though you conquer external foes, they will only increase.
> Therefore with the militia of love and compassion
> Subdue your own mind—
> This is the practice of bodhisattvas.
>
> Gyelsay Togmay Sangpo, *The Thirty-seven Practices of Bodhisattvas*

Patience is the ability to remain undisturbed in the face of harm or suffering. Being patient does not mean being passive. Rather, it gives us the clarity of mind necessary to act or not to act. Each of the following points is a different method of counteracting anger. Think of an example from your life of a time you were angry and practice looking at the situation from this new perspective.

1. Whether or not what the other person says is true, there is no reason to get angry when you are criticized. If what the other person says is true, it is like being told you have a nose. Both the other person and you know this is true, so there is no reason to be angry about it. You should simply acknowledge your mistake. On

the other hand, if someone blames you for something you didn't do, it is as if the person said you have horns on your head. There's no reason to be angry at something that is untrue.

2. Ask yourself, "Can I do something about it?" If you can, anger is out of place because you can improve the situation. If you can't, anger is useless because nothing can be done.

3. Examine how you got involved in the situation. This has two parts:

   - What actions did you do recently to prompt the disagreement? Examining this helps you understand why the other person is upset.
   - Recognize that unpleasant situations are due to your having harmed others earlier in this life or in previous lives. Seeing this as the principal cause, you can learn from past mistakes and resolve to act differently in the future.

4. Remember the kindness of a disagreeable person (enemy). First, he or she points out your mistakes so you can correct them and improve. Second, the enemy gives you the opportunity to practice patience, a necessary quality in your spiritual development. In these ways, the enemy is kinder to you than your friends or even the Buddha.

5. Instead of identifying with the self-centered attitude and thinking that it is you, see it as something separate from you. Then, recognizing it as the source of all your problems, give the pain to it, thinking, "Self-centered attitude, the negative karma that is now ripening as pain was created under your influence. Therefore, you should experience this pain, not me." In this way, mentally give the pain to the self-centered attitude.

6. Ask yourself, "Is it the person's nature to act like this?" If it is, there's no reason to be angry, for that would be like being annoyed with fire for burning. If it isn't the person's nature, anger is also unrealistic, for it would be like getting angry at the sky for having clouds in it.

7. Examine the disadvantages of anger and holding a grudge. Having done so, you will want to give them up because you want to be happy and they cause only suffering.

8. Recognize that it is the other person's unhappiness and confusion that make the

person harm you. Since you know what it's like to be unhappy, you can empathize and have compassion for the other person.

FAR-REACHING JOYOUS EFFORT

> What is joyous effort? It is enthusiasm for virtue.
> What is said to be its antithesis?
> It is spiritual sloth, clinging to the reprehensible,
> Apathy, and self-contempt.
> > Shantideva, *A Guide to the Bodhisattva's Way of Life*

Joyous effort is taking delight in what is virtuous and worthwhile. To cultivate it, we must counteract the three kinds of laziness:

1. procrastination and sleep. Do you put off Dharma study and practice? Do you sleep more than your body needs? Do you like to lie around and do nothing? If so, meditation on death will help you to not waste time being slothful.
2. attachment to worldly affairs and pleasures. Do you keep busy doing things or worrying about things which are not very important from a Dharma viewpoint? Are you attached to worldly success, worldly pleasures, and activities that are not very meaningful in the long run? If so, reflect on the disadvantages of cyclic existence. This will help you to see the futility of being attached to cyclic existence, invigorate your desire to be free from it, and enable you to set your priorities wisely.
3. discouragement and putting yourself down. Do you tend to be self-critical and judgmental? Do you have difficulties with self-esteem? Remember your Buddha nature and reflect on your precious human life. This will uplift your mind so you can recognize your potential.

Conclusion: Develop a sense of courage and joy so that you can engage in the three types of joyous effort:

1. withstanding discomfort to work for others' welfare (armorlike joyous effort)
2. doing all constructive action motivated by the altruistic intention
3. working to benefit others

FAR-REACHING CONCENTRATION

Realizing that one who is well endowed with insight through serenity
Eradicates mental afflictions,
One should first seek serenity.
Serenity is due to detachment toward the world and due to joy.
Shantideva, *A Guide to the Bodhisattva's Way of Life*

Concentration is the ability to focus single-pointedly on a constructive object. Unlike the other far-reaching practices, analytical meditation is not done with regard to far-reaching concentration. Instead, the points below are practiced to develop stabilizing or single-pointed meditation, which leads to serenity. You can apply the points when you practice stabilizing meditation, for example, on the breath or the visualized image of the Buddha. More explanation on the five faults is found in the chapter "Working with Distractions."

By examining your mind, notice when the five faults impeding concentration arise:

1. laziness: feeling that meditation is difficult and being reluctant to make the effort
2. forgetting the instructions on how to develop serenity or forgetting the object of meditation (your concentration on the object of meditation is not stable)
3. laxity (heaviness or unclarity) or excitement (distraction to an object of attachment)
4. not applying antidotes to the above faults
5. applying the antidotes when they are not needed

When one of the faults arises, apply its corresponding antidotes.

To counteract laziness:
1. confidence: knowing the benefits and results of serenity
2. aspiration: wishing to practice serenity
3. enthusiastic perseverance: having delight and eagerness to practice
4. flexibility: having serviceability of body and mind while meditating

To counteract forgetting the object of meditation:
5. mindfulness: remembering and staying on the object of meditation

To counteract distraction, laxity, or excitement by noticing their presence:
6. introspective alertness

To counteract not applying antidotes to the faults:
7. application of appropriate antidotes

To counteract applying antidotes when it is not necessary:
8. equanimity: refraining from applying antidotes when they are not needed

FAR-REACHING WISDOM

> Here "self" is an inherent existence of phenomena, that is, nondependence on another. The nonexistence of this is selflessness. This (selflessness) is realized as twofold through a division into persons and (other) phenomena—a selflessness of persons and a selflessness of (other) phenomena,
> Chandrakirti, *Commentary on (Aryadeva's)* Four Hundred

Wisdom is the ability to analyze what is virtuous and nonvirtuous as well as the ability to perceive emptiness, the lack of inherent existence of all persons and phenomena. Understanding dependent arising aids in understanding the emptiness of inherent or independent existence.

Dependent Arising

> When dependent arising is seen
> Ignorance will not occur.
> Thus every effort has been made here
> To explain precisely this subject.
> Aryadeva, *The Four Hundred*

All phenomena (including people) depend on other factors for their existence. They are dependent in three ways:

1. All the functioning things in our world arise depending on causes. Pick any object and reflect on the various causes and conditions that were necessary for it to come into existence. For example, a house exists because of so many non-house things that existed before it—building materials, designers and construction workers, etc.
2. Phenomena exist by depending on their parts. Mentally dissect a thing to discover all of the different parts that compose it. Each of these parts is again made of parts. For example, your body is made of many non-body things—limbs, organs, etc. Each of these, in turn, is composed of molecules, atoms, and subatomic particles.
3. Phenomena exist in dependence on their being conceived and given a name. For example, Tenzin Gyatso is the Dalai Lama because people conceived of that position and gave him that title.

Conclusion: Because nothing exists on its own, see that things are more fluid and dependent than you previously thought.

Emptiness

> If a person is not earth, not water,
> Not fire, not wind, not space,
> Not consciousness, and not all of them,
> What person is there other than these?
> Nagarjuna, *Precious Garland*

The four-point analysis for meditating on the emptiness of the person, oneself:

1. Identify the object of negation: an independent, solid, inherently existent person. Think of a time when you felt a strong emotion. How does the "I" appear at that time?
2. Establish the pervasion. If such an independent self existed, it would have to be either one and the same with the mental and physical aggregates or completely separate from them. There is no other alternative.
3. Examine all the parts of your body and all aspects of your mind. Are you any one of them? Determine that the "I" is not one and the same as the body or the mind, or a combination of the two.
4. Try to find a self that is independent from your body and mind. Can your body and mind be in one place and "I" in another? Determine that the self is not separate from the body and mind.

Conclusion: The self does not exist in the way you previously felt it did. Feel the lack of such an independent and solid self that needs to be defended.

The following meditation on how to rely on a spiritual mentor comes at the beginning of the traditional lamrim, which assumes that a person is already familiar with Buddhism. This is not the case for people who are new to Buddhism, however. Only after we have an idea of the general Buddhist view and aims—that we have gained from doing the preceding meditations—will we want to make a commitment to practice the path. In order to practice seriously and gain Dharma realizations, forming a healthy relationship with a spiritual mentor is essential.

HOW TO RELY ON A SPIRITUAL MENTOR

> When you rely on them your faults come to an end
> And your good qualities grow like the waxing moon.
> Cherish spiritual teachers
> Even more than your own body—
> This is the practice of bodhisattvas.
>
> > Gyelsay Togmay Sangpo, *The Thirty-seven Practices*
> > *of Bodhisattvas*

1. To progress on the path, it is important to rely on and be guided by qualified spiritual mentors. Think about why it is important to select teachers who have the following qualities:
   - stable practice or realization of the higher trainings of ethical conduct, meditative stabilization, and wisdom
   - vast and deep knowledge of the scriptures
   - joy and enthusiasm to teach
   - ability to express the teachings clearly
   - loving concern and compassion for the students
   - patience and willingness to undergo the difficulties of guiding others on the path

2. Consider the advantages of relying on a qualified teacher:
   - You will learn the correct teachings and know how to practice them properly.
   - You will gain realizations and approach enlightenment.
   - You will avoid unfortunate rebirths.
   - You won't lack spiritual teachers in your future lives.

3. Consider the disadvantages of not properly relying on a teacher:
   - None of the above benefits will accrue.
   - You will continue to wander in cyclic existence, especially in unfortunate rebirths.
   - Even though you may try to practice, your practice won't be successful.
   - Your good qualities will decline.

4. Practice relying on your teachers through your thoughts:
   - Develop faith and confidence in them by remembering their qualities and the role they play in your spiritual progress. They teach you exactly what the Buddha would teach you if he were here. They work to benefit you in the same way as the Buddha does. If you pick faults in your teachers, check whether the faults come from the teacher or instead are projections of your own mind.
   - Develop gratitude and respect by thinking of their kindness. You did not have the fortune to receive teachings directly from the Buddha or the great masters of the past. Due to the kindness of your spiritual mentors, you are able to listen to teachings, be inspired by their living example of the Dharma, take precepts, and receive guidance in your practice.

5. Practice relying on your teachers through your actions. You do this by:
   - making offerings to them
   - showing respect and offering your service to help them with various projects they do
   - practicing the teachings as they instructed

Conclusion: Make a determination to check a person's qualities before taking that person as your teacher. Determine to put effort into cultivating a relationship with your teachers that is imbued with faith, respect, and gratitude, so that you will progress easily and steadily on the path to enlightenment.

11. Additional Dedication Verses

In addition to the dedication verses at the conclusion of the meditation on the Buddha, you may also like to recite any or all of the following prayers. These dedications may also be done at the end of the day to dedicate the positive potential created by ourselves and others that day.

Dedication Prayer of
the Gradual Path to Enlightenment
by Je Tsongkhapa

From my two collections, vast as space, that I have amassed from working with effort at this practice for a great length of time, may I become the chief leading Buddha for all those whose mind's wisdom eye is blinded by ignorance.

Even if I do not reach this state, may I be held in your loving-compassion for all my lives, Manjushri. May I find the best of complete graded paths of the teachings, and may I please all the Buddhas by practicing well.

Using skillful means drawn by the strong force of compassion, may I clear the darkness from the minds of all beings with the points of the path as I have discerned them; may I uphold Buddha's teachings for a very long time.

With my heart going out with great compassion in whatever directions the most precious teachings have not yet spread, or once spread have declined, may I expose this treasure of happiness and aid.

May the minds of those who wish for liberation be granted bounteous peace, and the Buddhas' deeds be nourished for a long time by this gradual path to enlightenment completed due to the wondrous virtuous conduct of the Buddhas and their spiritual children.

May all human and nonhuman beings who eliminate adversity and make things conducive for practicing the excellent paths never be parted in any of their lives from the purest path praised by the Buddhas.

Whenever someone makes effort to act in accordance with the tenfold *Mahayana* virtuous practices, may he or she always be assisted by the mighty ones; and may oceans of prosperity spread everywhere.

DEDICATION FROM *GUIDE TO THE BODHISATTVA'S WAY OF LIFE*
by the great Indian sage Shantideva

> May all beings everywhere
> Plagued by sufferings of body and mind
> Obtain an ocean of happiness and joy
> By virtue of my merits.

> May no living creature suffer,
> Commit evil, or ever fall ill.
> May no one be afraid or belittled,
> With a mind weighed down by depression.

> May the blind see forms,
> And the deaf hear sounds.
> May those whose bodies are worn with toil
> Be restored on finding repose.

May the naked find clothing,
The hungry find food.
May the thirsty find water
And other delicious drinks.

May the poor find wealth,
Those weak with sorrow find joy.
May the forlorn find hope,
Constant happiness, and prosperity.

May all who are ill and injured
Quickly be freed from their ailments.
Whatever diseases there are in the world,
May these never occur again.

May the frightened cease to be afraid
And those bound be freed.
May the powerless find power
And may people think of benefiting each other.

For as long as space endures
And as long as living beings remain,
Until then may I too abide
To dispel the misery of the world.

Dedication for a Meaningful Life
by Zopa Rinpoche

Whatever actions I do—eating, walking, sitting, sleeping, working, and so forth—
and whatever I experience in life—up or down, happy or unhappy, healthy or sick,
whether I have a terminal disease or don't, whether my life is peaceful and harmo-

nious or with discord and difficulties, whether I am successful or fail, rich or poor, praised or criticized, loved or unloved, whether I am living or dying, or even born in a horrible rebirth, whether I live long or not—may my life be beneficial for all beings. The main purpose of my life is not simply to be rich, respected, famous, healthy, and peaceful. The meaning of my life is to benefit all sentient beings. Therefore, from now on, may whatever actions I do be beneficial for all sentient beings. May whatever I experience in life be dedicated to actualizing the path to enlightenment in my mind. May my actions and experiences cause all sentient beings to attain full enlightenment quickly.

PART III

Keeping on Track

12. OVERVIEW OF THE GRADUAL PATH TO ENLIGHTENMENT

I<small>N HIS TEXT</small> *Lamp of the Path*, Atisha, the great eleventh century Indian sage who headed the second transmission of Buddhism to Tibet, described three levels of spiritual practitioners, each with its own aspiration, method to cultivate that aspiration, and practices to do to actualize that aspiration once it has been cultivated. In this way he systematized the vast array of various teachings the Buddha gave so that newcomers as well as seasoned practitioners would know how to structure their practice in a step-by-step manner that leads to full enlightenment. Je Tsongkhapa and other Tibetan sages elaborated upon this, producing many texts on the stages of the path (also known as the gradual path). Having a good overview of this structure enables us to place any teaching we may hear into the larger framework of the path to enlightenment, thus helping us avoid confusion. This overview consists of a chart as well as a brief description of the purpose of each major topic in Je Tsongkhapa's *The Great Treatise on the Stages of the Path to Enlightenment* (*Lamrim Chenmo*, also translated as *The Great Treatise on the Gradual Path to Enlightenment*).

In the chart below, the three principal aspects of the path are in bold in order to show their relationship to the three levels of spiritual practitioners.

Level	Aspiration to develop	What to meditate on to develop it	What to practice once you have developed that aspiration
Path in common with initial level practitioners	To die peacefully and to have a good rebirth	Precious human life; impermanence and death; unfortunate realms of rebirth	Refuge, karma and its effects
Path in common with middle level practitioners	**Determination to be free from cyclic existence and attain liberation**	Four Noble Truths, the disadvantages of cyclic existence, the nature of afflictions, the factors that stimulate their arising	Three Higher Trainings: 1. Ethical conduct 2. Concentration 3. **Wisdom (correct view)**
Path of advanced level practitioners	**Altruistic intention (bodhicitta)**	Equanimity Seven point instruction of cause and result: 1. Recognizing all sentient beings as our parents 2. Remembering their kindness 3. Repaying their kindness 4. Love 5. Compassion 6. Great resolve 7. Bodhicitta Equalizing and exchanging self and others 1. Equalizing self and others 2. Disadvantages of self-centeredness 3. Benefits of cherishing others 4. Exchanging self and others 5. Taking and giving 6. Bodhicitta	Six far-reaching practices: 1. Generosity 2. Ethical conduct 3. Patience 4. Joyous effort 5. Meditative stabilization 6. **Wisdom** The four ways of gathering disciples: 1. Generosity 2. Pleasant speech 3. Encouraging them to practice 4. Acting accordingly oneself The path of tantra

The Purpose of Each Topic

While engaging in the study of an elaborate treatise such as *The Great Treatise on the Stages of the Path to Enlightenment* or on any of the smaller texts describing the gradual path to enlightenment, knowing the purpose and subtopics of each major topic is helpful. This enables us to know the principal understanding we want to derive from studying that major topic. This, in turn, helps us to see how all the topics and meditations fit together to form a systematic path to practice. The following is, therefore, a very brief overview of the topics in the order in which they are explained.

Developing confidence in the teachings and lineage of teachers

Preeminent qualities of the compilers

This section explains that the teachings come from a pure lineage of reliable practitioners who have actualized the results of the path that they teach. In this way, we develop confidence in the path and the possibility of realizing it ourselves.

Preeminent qualities of the teachings

This section describes how studying the gradual path will help us. We come to understand how all the various teachings can be organized into a gradual process that we can practice to become enlightened. This will help us to avoid sectarianism and confusion about how to practice.

How to engage with the teachings

Here we learn how the gradual path should be studied and taught; that is, how to select a qualified spiritual mentor, the qualities we should try to develop as a disciple or student, and how to listen to and teach the Dharma so that great benefit will ensue.

How to meditate on the stages of the path, with the example of the meditation on the spiritual mentor

Preparatory practices

This section lays out how to begin a meditation session so that we can prepare our mind to contemplate the lamrim topics listed below most effectively.

Relying on a spiritual teacher

Here we learn how to have healthy and constructive relationships with our spiritual mentors so that we will benefit from their guidance.

Appreciating your special opportunity

The qualities of a precious human life

This topic teaches us to recognize the positive situation we have so that we don't take it for granted. It helps us to abandon depression, make use of our opportunity, and generate joy and enthusiasm to practice.

The purpose of a precious human life

This section describes how to give deep and vast meaning to our lives by contemplating the goals towards which to direct our energy. This gives us a sense of confidence and enthusiasm to make our lives meaningful by using this opportunity for a noble purpose.

The rarity and difficulty of obtaining a precious human life

Seeing that our present opportunity is unique and hard to obtain, we feel even more inspired to use it wisely.

By having confidence in qualified teachers and confidence in our ability to practice because we have a precious human life, we can use these beneficial circumstances to practice the initial, middle, and advanced levels of the path to enlightenment.

The Path in Common with Initial Level Practitioners

This path is "common with initial level practitioners" because we do the same practice as they do, but our long-term motivation is the altruistic intention. Attaining a good rebirth is a necessary step in that direction, for without it we will lack the necessary circumstances in future lives to continue cultivating bodhicitta and practicing the bodhisattva path.

Advantages of remembering death and disadvantages of not doing so

Here we develop a healthy way of regarding death and understand how thinking constructively about our mortality helps us set our priorities wisely so that we and others will benefit in the long term.

Eight worldly concerns

We recognize how we waste our lives through attachment and aversion to transient pleasures and displeasures, resulting in more problems for ourselves in this and future lives. We develop the intention to avoid getting involved in the eight worldly concerns as much as possible because they only cause us problems in this and future lives and obstruct the path to enlightenment from developing in our mindstreams.

Actual meditation on death

This meditation enables us to discriminate what is important and what is unimportant to do while we are alive, to set our priorities in life clearly and with wisdom, and to prepare well for death so that when the time of death arrives, we will remain tranquil.

The possibility of unfortunate rebirth

We consider the states our minds could fall into if we keep on with our old bad habits and waste our potential.

Taking refuge in the Three Jewels

We develop the confidence and trust in the Three Jewels that come from knowing the qualities and abilities of the Buddha, Dharma, and Sangha to offer us positive direction and guidance in our lives.

Observing cause and effect (karma and its effects)

This topic describes the most essential and immediate way to avoid pain now and in the future. We can act to avoid creating the cause for suffering, to purify the harmful causes already created, and to create the causes for future happiness.

THE PATH IN COMMON
WITH INTERMEDIATE LEVEL PRACTITIONERS

This path is "common with intermediate level practitioners" because we do the same practices as they do, but our long-term motivation is the altruistic intention, not only our personal liberation from cyclic existence. We practice in accordance with their path because it is a necessary step in order to generate bodhicitta and practice the bodhisattva path, because without first seeing the disadvantages of and wishing to be free from our own cyclic existence, it is not possible to have this compassionate wish for others.

Four Noble Truths

Here we know the unsatisfactory nature of our cyclic existence, understand the causes that bring it about, aspire to actualize their cessation, and learn how to practice the path leading to nirvana, a state of true peace.

Disadvantages of cyclic existence

This meditation helps us gain the momentum to change and to remove our complacency through looking at the unsatisfactory conditions in which we live.

The causes of cyclic existence

We learn how to discriminate mental afflictions from beneficial attitudes and emotions and how the former keep us bound in cyclic existence. This increases our determination to be free from cyclic existence by ceasing its causes.

The path to liberation

This topic shows us the way to be released from cyclic existence by practicing the higher trainings in ethical conduct, concentration, and wisdom. (The latter two are discussed in depth in the path of the advanced level practitioner in order to emphasize that it is best to develop the altruistic intention and practice these trainings with that motivation.)

THE PATH OF
ADVANCED LEVEL PRACTITIONERS

In the initial and intermediate levels, we developed love and compassion for ourselves by reflecting on the unsatisfactory conditions of our cyclic existence. In the advanced level, we reflect on the unsatisfactory conditions of others' lives and develop great love, great compassion, and the great resolve to work for their benefit. This spurs us to generate bodhicitta, the altruistic intention to become a Buddha for the benefit of all sentient beings. When our bodhicitta is spontaneous, such that whenever we see any sentient being, our automatic reaction is "I want to become a Buddha in order to liberate them from suffering and lead them to enlightenment," we actually enter the bodhisattva path.

Advantages of the altruistic intention

This topic generates great enthusiasm in our mind to engage in the causal meditations that lead to the generation of love, compassion, and the altruistic intention.

Equanimity

Before we can love others equally, we must remove the hindrances of clinging attachment for friends, aversion towards people we don't like, and apathy for strangers. Meditation on equanimity enables us to do this and to generate an openhearted attitude that cares equally about each sentient being.

Bodhicitta may be cultivated by two methods: the seven-point instruction of cause and effect, or equalizing and exchanging self and others.

The seven-point instruction of cause and effect
for generating the altruistic intention:

1. recognizing all sentient beings as having been our parents
   This leads us to have a sense of our long and intimate connection with others throughout many previous lives.
2. remembering their kindness
   We understand the benefit we have received from others so that we let go of defensiveness and see others as lovable.
3. repaying their kindness
   When we realize the great benefits we have received from others, a deeply felt wish to repay their kindness naturally arises.
4. heartwarming love
   Here we train our minds and hearts to see all sentient beings as lovable.
5. compassion
   Now we generate the unbiased wish for all sentient beings to be free from all unsatisfactory conditions and their causes.
6. great resolve
   Doing this meditation, we take responsibility and act in order to bring about our loving and compassionate aspirations for others.
7. altruistic intention
   The effect of the six preceding meditations is the intention to become a fully enlightened Buddha in order to be of most effective benefit to others.

Equalizing and exchanging self and other

1. equalizing self and others

   We train ourselves to look beyond superficial differences and recognize that we and others are the same in wanting to be happy and to be free from pain.

2. the disadvantages of self-centeredness

   Instead of feeling guilty because we are selfish, we recognize that although the self-centered attitude pretends to look out for our welfare, in fact it deceives us and underlies all our conflict and pain.

3. the advantages of cherishing others

   We learn to cherish others sincerely by recognizing that such an attitude is the source of all our own and others' happiness. (This is very different from pleasing others because we want them to like or approve of us.)

4. exchanging self and others

   Seeing that selfishly caring only for ourselves causes us constant unhappiness and frustration and that cherishing others brings only benefit and happiness to ourselves and others, we practice shifting the primary object of our care from ourselves to others.

5. taking and giving

   We train in gladly taking the dukkha that others don't want and using it to destroy what we don't want—our own ignorance and self-centeredness. We also practice joyfully transforming our body, possessions, and positive potential so that they become whatever others need and to give them to others with delight, free from hesitation or miserliness.

6. altruistic intention

   The primary intention for everything we do is to become a fully enlightened Buddha in order to be of most effective benefit to others.

Taking the bodhisattva vows

Here we determine to engage in the practices of a bodhisattva: the six far-reaching practices and the four ways of gathering students.

The six far-reaching practices:

1. generosity
   This is the wish to give our body, possessions, and positive potential to others for their benefit. We develop joy in giving these.
2. ethical conduct
   We gain a firm determination not to harm others physically, verbally, or mentally.
3. patience
   To benefit others, bodhisattvas need the ability to remain undisturbed and calm when faced with harm or suffering.
4. joyous effort
   By taking delight in acting constructively, we practice the path joyfully.
5. meditative stabilization
   The ability to direct the mind to whatever positive object we wish, for as long as we wish, without physical or mental discomfort, is essential to realizing the ultimate nature of reality and rooting out the afflictions.
6. wisdom
   By correctly understanding both the conventional functioning of things as well as their deeper mode of existence—the emptiness of inherent existence—we will gradually eradicate all obscurations from our mindstream and gain great abilities to benefit all sentient beings.

The four ways of gathering disciples:

1. generosity
   People will be attracted to us by our generosity and want to follow Dharma instructions.
2. pleasant speech
   According to their disposition and interest, we teach sentient beings the Dharma and give them useful Dharma advice.

3. encouraging others to practice

   We skillfully encourage others to practice the Dharma.

4. acting according to what we instruct others to do

   In order to be a good role model and to inspire others to practice, we must "walk our talk" without behaving hypocritically.

The tantric path

Because of our wish to quickly become a Buddha for the benefit of others, we assume tantric vows and commitments and receive initiation into a tantric practice. Then we practice the special tantric techniques to purify our mind and create positive potential, to develop concentration and wisdom, and to create the causes for the body and mind of a Buddha.

13. WORKING WITH DISTRACTIONS

STABILITY AND CLARITY are two main qualities of good meditation. With stability, the mind remains on the meditation object; with clarity, the mind is bright and alert. To the extent that both qualities are present, our meditation is that much more concentrated and penetrative.

Our ability to meditate requires training and patience and develops gradually. Like any other skill, such as reading or playing music, meditation takes time, effort, and persistence to develop. In addition, we face and must overcome certain challenges along the way—the five hindrances and the five faults. Fortunately, the Buddha taught precise methods for doing this.

THE FIVE HINDRANCES

In many sutras the Buddha spoke of the five hindrances to developing serenity (*shamatha*). For example, in the "Maggasamyutta" in the *Samyutta Nikaya*, he said:

> Monastics, there are these five hindrances. What five? The hindrance of sensual desire, the hindrance of ill will, the hindrance of sloth and torpor, the hindrance of restlessness and remorse, the hindrance of doubt. These

are the five hindrances. This Noble Eightfold Path is to be developed for direct knowledge of these five hindrances, for the full understanding of them, for their utter destruction, for their abandoning.

1. Sensual desire

Sensual desire is a type of attachment that is directed primarily at objects of the senses: sights, sounds, smells, tastes, and tactile objects. It may also include mental objects, for example attachment to a good reputation, to being right, to receiving praise. We can spend hours sitting in perfect meditation posture with our mind focused not on a wholesome object, but on a sense object as we daydream how wonderful it would be to have it.

While the wisdom realizing emptiness is the general antidote for all the hindrances, we need to use specific ones that are initially easier to practice for each hindrance. Here, the antidote for sensual desire is reflecting on impermanence and on the undesirable aspects of whatever we are craving. Antidotes for specific objects are discussed in more detail in Chapter 14, "Antidotes to the Mental Afflictions."

The usage of the word "desire" can be confusing, because in English "desire" has several different meanings. One is sensual desire, which is the translation of the Pali word *kamacchanda*. This type of desire prevents liberation, causes suffering, and is to be abandoned on the path. However, the English word "desire" may also have the connotation of "positive aspiration" as in "I desire to develop impartial love and compassion for all beings" or "She desires to become a better person." This type of desire is not a type of attachment; it is not an impediment on the path. Rather it is helpful because it aspires for what is wholesome and beneficial.

Understanding this is important for in the past some people have written books based on misinterpretations of the Buddha's meaning. Thus some people think, "The goal of Buddhism is to go beyond all desire so therefore enlightenment is like being a bump on a log. I just sit there not wanting anything, not caring about anything." This is totally incorrect. To the contrary, practitioners cultivate positive aspirations or desires and then set about creating the causes to actualize them. They desire to eliminate sensual desire because it keeps them bound in a cycle of dissatisfaction and misery.

2. Ill will

Ill will may take many forms, for example resentment, holding a grudge, wishing that others have problems, malicious thoughts, or plotting revenge. This clearly interrupts meditation and it also prompts negative actions during our daily life. The antidotes are the cultivation of patience, compassion, and forgiveness.

3. Sloth and torpor

Dullness and sleepiness are a big hindrance to meditation. We may be wide awake when our mind is filled with gossip and a moment later be dull and sleepy when directing our mind to a wholesome meditation object. Sleepiness in meditation often has nothing to do with not having gotten enough sleep. Rather it is a defense used by our self-centered attitude to prevent us from getting to know ourselves and from practicing the Dharma. If you have problems with sloth and sleepiness, do prostrations before the meditation session. Putting cold water on your face and arms prior to sitting is also helpful. Don't eat a heavy meal before meditating and take off clothes that make you excessively warm. Being a little cool will keep your mind alert. Sit up straight. Make sure your eyes are a little open; the light entering will prevent dullness.

During mindfulness of breathing try adding the following visualization to counteract dullness: Imagine as you exhale that the dullness and foggy-mindedness leave you in the form of smoke, which then vanishes completely. As you inhale, think that the breath is the nature of light and this light fills your entire body and mind. Doing this for several minutes can dispel dullness.

If that fails, the masters recommend going to sit near the edge of a high place—for example, on a roof, near a cliff. That should dispel the sleepiness. However, if you're still drowsy, don't stay there—you might get hurt!

4. Restlessness and remorse

Both restlessness and remorse distract us from the meditation object. A restless mind is one filled with worry and anxiety. Prevalent in modern society, these emotions cause a lot of distress and are related to fear. When researching these emotions, we may discover that attachment lies behind them. That is, we are attached to someone or something and worry about losing it, being separated from it, its being harmed, and so forth. Such worry and anxiety are particularly useless because they focus on a problem that hasn't even happened yet! Ruminating on "what if . . ." is an excellent way to make ourselves miserable. When such a mental habit starts playing, pushing the pause button and returning to what is happening now is the best antidote. Sometimes we can even learn to laugh at the silliness of our worries.

Remorse distracts the mind as well. There are two types of remorse, one that is useful on the path, the other that isn't. Remorse in the form of regret for negative actions is a necessary element to purify negative karma. However, it's better not to create that karma to start with. Thus this kind of remorse is eliminated by practicing ethical conduct as a preventative measure.

Another type of remorse is similar to guilt, which is not at all useful on the Dharma path. Guilt keeps us focused on ourselves in an unhealthy way. It is supported by the misconception, "The worse I feel, the more I'm atoning for my mistaken actions." This way of thinking is silly for it leads to depression and makes us stuck. It also overemphasizes our importance because we accept responsibility for what isn't our responsibility and subconsciously think, "I'm so important I can make everything go wrong." Analyzing what is and isn't our responsibility helps in freeing ourselves from guilt. Generating healthy regret that leads us to do purification practices also remedies it.

5. Doubt

There are various types of doubt that may distract us during meditation and plague our mind in general. The Tibetans have a saying, "You can't sew with a two-pointed needle." Similarly, we can't get anywhere when the mind is filled with doubt.

Doubt may concern important philosophical topics, and resolving it is necessary in order to have the first aspect of the Eightfold Noble Path, correct view. Doubt is different from curiosity and open-minded exploration, for doubt simply makes our mind twirl around uselessly. This kind of doubt isn't really looking for a resolution, it just chatters away, "How do you know this? Can you prove that?" Curiosity, on the other hand, sparks us to actively seek the means to understand a topic. With curiosity, we ask questions and then reflect on the answers using our intelligence to develop accurate understanding. An antidote for the chattering doubt is to focus one-pointedly on the breath and the physical sensations accompanying it.

Another kind of doubt is doubting ourselves, our capabilities, and our activities. This fills the mind with thoughts such as, "Am I capable of meditating? Will this accomplish anything positive? Is this the right practice to do? Maybe I should do another practice or follow another path?" This doubt, too, functions to waste time and energy by creating unnecessary confusion in the mind. It is deceptive in that we often don't recognize it as doubt, but fully believe the truth of what we are thinking. A little slogan is helpful to remember in such situations: Don't believe everything you think! This slogan is good to recall in instances of sensual desire, ill will, worry, and guilt. Asking ourselves, "Does what I'm thinking correspond with how things are?" invokes our discerning wisdom and thus calms the mind from the disruptions caused by the mental afflictions.

WHEN TO APPLY ANTIDOTES TO HINDRANCES

When we are meditating and thoughts, sensations, sounds, and so forth enter our field of awareness, the first strategy is to bring our focus back to the object of meditation. If the distraction is weak, this usually works. However, sometimes the distracting thought or emotion is very strong and our mind returns to it repeatedly. In this case, we need to temporarily shift the object of our meditation to the antidote to that affliction. For example, if ill will arises in our mind, we try coming back to the object of meditation, which could be the breath, the image of the Buddha, or the specific lamrim topic on which we are meditating. But if the ill will continues to arise and our mind is under its power, then we have to leave our object of meditation temporarily and instead meditate on patience, love, and compassion. Some of these meditations are briefly outlined in the chapter "Antidotes to the Mental Afflictions."

They are described more extensively in *Working with Anger*. Once anger has subsided, patience is established, and our mind has become more tolerant and benevolent, we return to our initial meditation object.

THE FIVE FAULTS AND EIGHT ANTIDOTES

Maitreya, in his treatise *Differentiation of the Middle and the Extremes* (*Madhyantavibhanga*), described five faults that interrupt the cultivation of concentration and serenity. These are: 1) laziness, 2) forgetting the object of meditation, 3) laxity and excitement, 4) non-application of antidotes, and 5) over-application of the antidote. Fortunately, there are eight antidotes to counteract them: 1) confidence or faith, 2) aspiration, 3) effort, 4) pliancy, 5) mindfulness, 6) introspective alertness, 7) application of the antidote, and 8) equanimity. When meditating, try to recognize the obstacles in your mind when they occur and then apply their respective antidotes. Let's review these in more depth.

1. Laziness

Laziness in this case means feeling meditation is too difficult and being reluctant to make sustained effort in the practice. In the early stages of practice, laziness impedes us from getting to the meditation cushion, let alone beginning a meditation session. The first four antidotes, which are developed consecutively, are used to overcome laziness. These are:

- confidence or faith. By remembering the advantages of meditating and the disadvantages of letting the mind do whatever it wants, develop confidence in the practice.
- aspiration. By having confidence, wish to practice in order to realize the fruits of meditation.
- effort. By being confident and aspiring to practice, joyfully and enthusiastically make effort in your practice.

- pliancy. The fruit of effort, pliancy is the fitness and flexibility of body and mind that make meditation natural, pleasant, and easy.

2. Forgetting the object of meditation

After we have overcome laziness and sit down to meditate, the next fault that plagues us is forgetting the object of meditation. That is, the mind has wandered off. Forgetting the object of meditation could also come about because we have forgotten the instructions on how to do the meditation.

The antidote to forgetting the object of meditation is mindfulness, which is a mental factor that remembers the meditation object in such a way that distraction is prevented. In the breathing meditation, the object of meditation is the breath. In meditation involving visualization, it is the visualized object. In analytical meditation, the object of meditation is the topic you are examining. By listening to instructions, learn what the object of meditation is and have some understanding of it before you start. Then place your mindfulness on it and make a strong determination to keep it there.

3. Laxity and excitement

Although laxity and excitement are different, introspective alertness (vigilance) is the antidote to both. This is an introspective part of the mind that acts like a spy and notices if your concentration is sagging or has strayed.

When the mind is lax, lethargic, or drowsy, here are some suggestions on what to do:

- Visualize exhaling the drowsy, dull mind in the form of smoke, which then disappears. Imagine inhaling mindfulness, concentration, and cheerfulness in the form of bright light that fills your body and mind.
- If your object of meditation is a visualized object, make the object brighter or review the details of the visualization.
- Imagine a bright light at the point between the eyebrows. Light beams radiate from that and fill your entire body and mind, dispelling all drowsiness.

- Think about something that uplifts the mind, for example, the purpose and rarity of a precious human life, your great fortune at having the opportunity to meditate and develop your good qualities, Buddha potential, or the qualities of the Three Jewels.
- In general, strengthen your concentration on the object.
- Sprinkle water on your face.
- If the mind is very dull, conclude the session, take a walk in the fresh air, and gaze out into the distance. When you feel refreshed, return to meditate.
- Before you begin a meditation session, bow to the Three Jewels many times. This may be done while reciting the practice of the Thirty-five Buddhas, "The Bodhisattvas' Confession of Ethical Downfalls."
- Get enough exercise and change your diet. For example, do not eat meat and avoid greasy food.
- Turn down the heat in the room or remove warm clothing. Being cool and in a room that is not stuffy helps the mind not to be dull.

When the mind is excited and distracted towards objects of attachment, try one of the following suggestions:

- Gently, yet firmly, bring your concentration back to the meditation object.
- In the case of visualization or analytical meditations, do the breathing meditation for a while to calm the mind. Then return to the previous meditation object.
- Contemplate impermanence and death: death is certain, the time of death is uncertain, and when we die only our karmic latencies and mental habits come with our mindstream. Since our body, wealth, reputation, and loved ones are left behind, what use is letting our mind wander in attachment towards them? It is more worthwhile to practice the Dharma.
- Think about something that makes the mind more sober, for example, the defects of whatever it is you're attached to, the disadvantages of attachment, and so forth.

4. Non-application of antidotes

Laxity or excitement has arisen and for whatever reason, we do not try to counter-act it. The seventh antidote is applied here, that is, to apply the appropriate antidote.

5. Over-application of the antidote

In this case, rather than not apply the antidote, we over-apply it, cultivating the antidote when a fault has already been subdued and concentration has returned to the object of meditation. The eighth antidote, equanimity, addresses this situation. It enables the mind to remain tranquil and cease applying the antidote when it is no longer needed.

WORKING WITH PAIN

Most people at one time or another experience physical pain while meditating. Our mind has been born into a body that is under the influence of mental afflictions and karma, so of course this body will be uncomfortable to a greater or lesser degree. That's part of its nature. Physical pain is simply a sensation. However, aversion and fear arise in reaction to it, and they bring on mental pain, because our mind creates stories: We fear, "If I don't move my leg, I will be forever paralyzed!" or we become angry, "I can't stand this pain in my back another instant!" Then we whine, complain, feel sorry for ourselves, and hate whoever "invented" meditation.

In these cases, we are confusing the mental pain with the physical pain and suffer even more. When we recognize these two as separate, we are able to experience the physical sensation without our mind creating a reactive story about it.

Here are some ideas on how to "play" with painful sensations:

- Observe the pain. Is it fixed in one place? Does it have borders? Does it change or does it fluctuate? Study the pain and try to understand exactly where and what it is.

- Observe the physical sensation. What is painful about this sensation? Can you distinguish the sensation itself from the pain?
- Separate the physical sensation from your mental aversion to it. Which is more disturbing, the physical sensation or the mental aversion to it?
- Observe the stories your mind creates about the pain: Pain is unfair; it is unendurable; it will result in terrible, irreversible consequences, and so forth. Step back and observe, "Is that story correct? Will that really happen?" Let your mind relax and be free from worry, fear, and anger.
- Think, "The pain is here; there is no way around it. I will accept it and continue on."
- With concern, love, and compassion for all other beings, think, "May my experiencing this pain suffice for the pain and confusion of all other beings."

Some people find it helpful to set a determination of a reasonable period of time during which they will sit in meditation without moving. If you do this, do not make it into a contest in which you grit your teeth in pain just to say that you sat without moving for a certain length of time. That isn't conducive for focusing with wisdom on the object of meditation. On the other hand, avoid moving whenever you feel the slightest bit of restlessness or discomfort. Doing that isn't conducive for developing concentration either. Rather, note when there is the urge to move but don't move. Observe the sensation: Is it really pain or is it simply restless energy in the body? Learn to differentiate between these two. Learn, also, to differentiate between pain and discomfort. Watch and study both of those when they arise in your field of experience.

In general, when attachment, anger, jealousy, or other distracting emotions arise, observe them without getting involved in their stories. Experience the feeling, rather than repeat the story to yourself again and again. Be aware of what it feels like in your body when you are angry, jealous, arrogant, or clingy. Be aware of the feeling tone in your mind when one of these emotions is present. Observe how the feeling changes, never remaining the same.

Another strategy when distracting thoughts arise in meditation is gently to observe: Where is the thought? Does it have color or shape? Be aware if the thought arises, abides, and disappears without changing or if it changes in each moment. Subtly explore, without making it a topic of intellectual speculation: Where did this thought come from? Where does it exist now? Where does it go when it vanishes?

It is important to avoid criticizing yourself when your mind is distracted or dull. Do not fall into discouraging thoughts or self-hatred because these are unproductive and are to be abandoned on the path. Remember that internal transformation takes time and rejoice in your opportunity to learn and practice the Dharma. "Slowly, slowly," as Lama Thubten Yeshe used to say. Learn to be satisfied with what you are able to do now while you aspire to improve in the future.

14. Antidotes to the Mental Afflictions

B ECAUSE THE MIND is complex and the mental afflictions are deeply rooted, one type of meditation alone will not suffice for immediately purifying all mental afflictions and generating all good qualities. While direct perception of the emptiness of inherent existence—the nature of reality—is the ultimate antidote that has the power to eliminate the mental afflictions from their root, it takes time to cultivate the correct view of emptiness. In the meantime, we can benefit from knowing and applying the antidotes specific for each affliction. This chapter explains some of the most common and effective antidotes. It is by no means definitive, and you may add more disadvantages and antidotes as you learn or discover them. For a more complete explanation of the antidotes, refer to books on the gradual path (lamrim) and thought training (*lojong*). Many of these are listed in "Suggested Reading."

To apply an antidote, we must first be able to recognize the affliction when it is present in our mind. For that reason, the definition of each affliction is included. When we recognize an affliction in our mind, we must then be cognizant of its disadvantages, for without this we won't be motivated to free our minds from it. Thus some of the disadvantages of each affliction are listed. Deeply contemplating these disadvantages by making many examples from our lives pulls us out of the mental state that is stuck in that affliction.

Being aware of the disadvantages of an affliction, we then want to contemplate an antidote, that is, another way of viewing the situation that opposes that affliction and lessens its power. By making ourselves familiar with the disadvantages of and antidotes to each affliction through regular meditation, we will easily be able to recall them when an affliction has arisen in our mind. The emotion or attitude that is the direct opposite of each affliction is also listed. When, through applying an antidote, your mind is subdued and this new emotion or attitude is present, you will know that your mind has been transformed.

The definition and disadvantages of each affliction and the antidotes to it have been listed in a concise, bulleted form for use in your meditation practice. When your mind is afflicted, you can easily read them and select the particular antidote to that affliction that will help you at that moment. This allows you to stay with your own experience without being "distracted" by a lengthy description of each antidote or stories of others' experiences applying them.

One day one antidote to a certain affliction easily enables you to let it go, while a month later another antidote may work more effectively. Thus it's wise to become familiar with all the antidotes to that affliction by meditating on them when your mind is not overwhelmed by that affliction. This will build up the habit of seeing situations in a new light so that when an affliction arises, you will more easily be able to change your interpretation of the event.

Time is needed to become deeply familiar with each antidote. In the heat of anger, don't expect your mind to become pacified simply by reading the list of antidotes to anger. Psychologists speak of a refractory period, during which a person experiencing an intense negative emotion is not receptive to any new information or to changing their perspective. Being aware of the disadvantages of a harmful emotion can shorten this refractory period. We must then apply an antidote with which we are very familiar to subdue that emotion.

While most of the antidotes listed here involve some sort of thinking in order to change our perspective, sometimes it is helpful simply to observe our experience of an emotion. For example, when anger arises, sit down and observe the sensations in your body and mind. What physical sensations accompany the anger? Observe your heartbeat, your stomach, the palms of your hands, and the kind of physical energy in your body. Observe the mood or "flavor" of your mind. Just feel the mental and physical sensations without reacting to them. After some time you may notice that the emotion is no longer there. That is because it is impermanent by nature. A negative emotion only lasts a long time when we ruminate about the story we tell ourselves about the situation. When we don't feed the story and instead remain focused on our experience, the disturbing emotion subsides because it is transient.

Don't expect your jealousy, for example, to vanish because you successfully applied the antidote once. Until we have realized emptiness directly and nonconceptually, afflictions will continue to arise in our mind. Don't be discouraged. Keep practicing. Making effort to transform our mind produces only benefit for ourselves and others.

ATTACHMENT

What is attachment?

Attachment is a mental factor that, based on overestimating or exaggerating the attractiveness of an object (a person, thing, idea, feeling, one's reputation, etc.), takes a strong interest in it and wishes to possess it. It sees the desired object as permanent, providing pleasure, pure, and self-existent (existing in and of itself, with an independent nature).

Detachment is an attitude that counteracts attachment. It withdraws our mind from its compulsive involvement with the object by understanding its nature and eliminates grasping to possess it.

What are the disadvantages of attachment?

1. It breeds dissatisfaction. We can't enjoy what we have and are continually dissatisfied, wanting more and better.
2. We go up and down emotionally.
3. We have many unrealistic expectations of other people and do not accept them for what they are.

4. We connive and plot to get what we want. We act hypocritically with ulterior motivations.
5. Even if we exert great effort over a long time to get the objects of attachment, we're not assured success.
6. We waste our life: we don't practice Dharma because we are distracted or obsessed by objects of attachment. Even if we try to practice Dharma, attachment continually interferes, distracting us from the practices to cultivate constructive qualities.
7. Our Dharma practice may become impure, because we give the appearance of practicing, but are really looking for reputation, offerings, or power.
8. Attachment is one of the principal obstacles to developing concentration.
9. We create much negative karma through stealing, coveting, and so forth.
10. It causes worry, anxiety, and frustration.
11. It causes us to have an unfortunate rebirth in the future and is the chief cause for samsara in general.
12. It causes us to have attachment in future lives.
13. It prevents us from having realizations and gaining liberation or enlightenment.
14. When we're parted from dear ones, our minds are tormented by sadness and grief. When we're with them, there's still no satisfaction.
15. We measure our success or failure as a person according to superficial factors such as material success and societal prestige.
16. We become confused because we don't know what to choose in our struggle to eke out the most happiness from every situation.
17. Attachment is involved in codependency and causes us to feel powerless because we give our power to those who have control over what we're attached to.
18. Attachment is closely related to and is a cause of fear. We fear not getting what we crave. We fear being separated from the people and objects we desire.

What are the antidotes to attachment?

1. Remember the disadvantages of attachment and the advantages of abandoning it.
2. Consider the ugly or impure aspect of the object.

3. Remember the impermanence of the object. Since it changes moment by moment and we'll eventually have to separate from it, what is the use of clinging to it now?

4. Think of our death and remember how objects of attachment are of no benefit to us at that time and may even be harmful.

5. Ask yourself, "Even if I get what I like, will it bring me ultimate and lasting happiness?"

6. Remember that we have had similar pleasures infinite times in past lives and it hasn't gotten us anywhere.

7. Mentally dissect the object or person into its parts and try to find what it is that seems so desirable about it.

8. Consider how our mind creates the beautiful object by interpreting it a certain way and giving it the label "beautiful." Then we confuse our concept of the object with the object itself.

Antidotes to attachment to praise and approval

1. When someone praises you, think the words are directed to a person behind you or to your spiritual master visualized in your heart.

2. Think, "Someone torturing me doesn't cause me to take unfortunate rebirths, but attachment to praise does."

3. Recall that other people are difficult to please. They may praise us now, but later may be jealous or competitive. They get angry when we don't agree with them. Therefore, what's the use of being attached to their praise and approval?

4. Praise can lead to pride, which is a huge obstacle to Dharma practice.

5. Praise doesn't bring us positive potential for future lives, long life, strength, good health, or comfort. It doesn't increase our love and compassion or help our Dharma practice. So what use is it?

6. When their sand castles collapse, children howl in despair. Similarly, we despair and complain when the praise and reputation we receive decrease.

7. Someone praising us doesn't mean we possess the qualities they say we have. A more reliable way to develop self-confidence is by understanding our potential to become a fully enlightened being.

8. Attached to praise, we allow other people to manipulate us. We abandon the discriminating wisdom that can discern who is trustworthy and who is not.
9. Praise does not benefit us; it helps the person who gives it. For example, when we praise Buddhas and great practitioners, do they benefit from it? No, we do.
10. When we have the quality that is being praised, remember that it is not ours. We have that good quality due to the kindness of those who raised us and taught us.
11. The person who praises us could criticize us five minutes later.
12. We can't take the praise with us when we die.
13. Sweet words are like an echo. Just as an echo depends on rocks, wind, vibration, and so on, the words praising me depend on many factors.
14. Analyze each word to see if happiness can be found within it. The pleasure we feel from being praised does not exist in the words, in the person who said them, or in us. It arises dependent on many conditions.

Antidotes to sexual attachment

It is important to note that the body and sex are not considered evil in Buddhism. The body is simply what it is, a collection of physical substances. Sexual intercourse is a biological function. However, when sexual attachment is rampant in the mind, engaging in stabilizing and analytical meditation becomes difficult. To increase our ability to concentrate on the object of meditation, applying any of the following antidotes is helpful.

1. Recall the difficulties that accompany romantic attachment. For example, we easily get involved in arrangements, games, and hassles in the process of establishing a relationship. Once we are in a relationship, quarrels, jealousy, possessiveness, and demands ensue. The other person is never totally satisfied with us and we are never completely satisfied with him or her.
2. Relationships must always end. It is impossible always to be together. As soon as there is coming together, then there must be separation.
3. Imagine the person when he or she was a baby or imagine what he or she will look like at age eighty. Alternatively, think of him or her as a brother or sister.

4. The body is like a factory producing impure substances and odors. Everything that comes out of the body—excrement, ear wax, mucus, and so forth—is unattractive. What is attractive about that?

5. Examine the insides of the body. If we don't desire it when the skin has been stripped away, why desire it when it's covered with skin?

6. Food is clean, but when it's chewed, it becomes unclean. The body is filled with partially digested food and excrement.

7. Why decorate a body which, if left in its natural state, would have bad breath, body odor, and wild hair?

8. Imagine the person's dead body. We have no desire to fondle that body then.

9. If we're frightened by a skeleton, shouldn't we be equally frightened by a walking corpse?

10. Our own bodies are sacks of unclean substances. What is the use, then, of being obsessed about touching and possessing another's body which is also made of such substances?

11. If we like to hug someone because his or her body is soft, why not hug a pillow?

12. If we say we love someone's mind, that cannot be touched.

13. If we don't like to touch excrement, why do we want to touch the body that produces it?

14. There may be some temporary pleasure from sexual relations, but it ends quickly and we're back where we began.

Anger

What is anger?

Anger (hostility) is a mental factor which, in reference to one of three objects, agitates the mind through being unable to bear the object or through intending to cause it harm. The three objects are the person or object that harms us, the suffering we receive, or the reason we are harmed. The word "anger" here includes a spectrum of emotions, including irritation, annoyance, resentment, grudge holding, spite, vengeance, rage, and so forth.

Patience is a mental state that counteracts anger. It is the ability to remain stead-fast and calm in the face of suffering or harm. There are three types of patience: 1) the patience that refrains from retaliation, 2) the patience that is able to endure suf-fering, and 3) the patience to practice the Dharma and challenge our misconcep-tions.

What are the disadvantages of anger and hostility?

1. One moment of anger destroys a great amount of the positive potential that we have created with so much effort.
2. We become disagreeable and bad tempered and are often in a bad mood.
3. Anger ruins friendships, generates tension with colleagues, and is the main cause for wars and conflicts.
4. Anger makes us unhappy, and we say and do things that make others—especially the people we care about the most—unhappy.
5. It robs us of our reason and good sense and makes us act outrageously, saying and doing things that later cause us to feel ashamed.
6. Under its influence, we harm others, physically and mentally.
7. Because we act so poorly, others do not like us and may even wish us ill.
8. We'll be quick to lose our temper again in future lives
9. We create much negative karma, causing us to be reborn in a place with much animosity, violence, and fear.
10. It impedes our spiritual advancement, and we are unable to attain realizations. In particular, it harms our cultivation of love and compassion and prevents us from becoming a bodhisattva.
11. Others may do what we want out of fear, but they neither love nor respect us. Is that what we want?

What are antidotes to it?

1. Remember the disadvantages of anger and the advantages of abandoning it.
2. Why be unhappy and angry if we can change a situation? Why be unhappy and angry if the situation cannot be remedied?

The patience of refraining from retaliation: antidotes to anger
arising when we have been harmed or threatened

1. We have problems and are harmed by another person because we created the cause in the past by harming others. Therefore, why be angry with the other person? It is only our own selfish mind and afflictions that are to blame. If we had exerted effort in the past to attain liberation or enlightenment, we would not be in this predicament now.

2. The other person is unhappy and that is why he is harming us. Recognize his suffering. Unhappy people should be objects of our compassion, not of our anger.

3. The person harming us is under the control of his afflictions, so why be angry with him?

4. If harmfulness were the nature of the other person, why be angry with her? We are not angry at fire for burning, because that is its nature. If harmfulness is not the nature of the other person, why be angry? We are not angry at the sky when it rains because storm clouds are not its nature.

5. Remember our faults. Our careless or inconsiderate actions in this life may have stimulated the problem.

6. If we give up the attachment to material possessions, friends and relatives, and our body, we will not be angry when they are harmed.

7. When people accurately mention our faults, they are saying what is true and what many other people have observed, so why be angry with them? It's like someone stating a fact, such as, "There is a nose on your face." Everyone sees it, so why try to deny it? Besides, they are giving us a chance to correct our faults and to improve ourselves.

8. If we are blamed unjustly, there is no reason to be angry because the other person is misinformed. We do not get angry if someone says we have a horn on our head because we know it is not true.

9. By retaliating, we create more negative karma to experience more problems in the future. Bearing the difficulty consumes our previously created negative karma.

10. The other person is creating negative karma by harming us and will reap the results of his actions. Therefore, he should be the object of compassion, not anger.

11. Mentally dissect the person or situation into parts and search for exactly what it is that is so distasteful.

12. See how our own mind creates the enemy by interpreting the situation in a certain way and giving the labels "bad" and "enemy."

12. The mental state that wants to retaliate and inflict pain on others is dreadful. There already is enough suffering in the world. Why create more?

14. Harming others and taking delight in causing them pain crushes our own self-respect.

15. There is no reason to get angry with someone who criticizes the Triple Gem or our Dharma teacher. She is only doing so out of ignorance. Her criticism does not harm the Triple Gem at all.

16. Remember the kindness of the enemy for giving us the opportunity to practice patience, for without it, we cannot attain enlightenment. Patience can only be practiced with an enemy. We cannot practice patience with the Buddha or our friends; therefore the enemy is rare and special.

17. If we are Dharma practitioners, there is no sense in relying upon the Buddha yet continuing to harm sentient beings. We not only become hypocrites, but also harm sentient beings whom the Buddha cherishes more than himself.

18. If we are kind to others, they will like and help us even now. In the end, the practice of patience will lead us to attain enlightenment.

19. Think, "Both this person I find so disagreeable and I are impermanent and empty of inherent existence."

20. Remember the person's kindness to you in past lives and think, "I must care for him with love now."

The patience of voluntarily enduring suffering:
antidotes to anger arising when we are suffering

1. Remember that the nature of cyclic existence is unsatisfactory. Pain and problems come naturally. There is nothing surprising about, for example, getting sick.
2. Reflect on the advantages of experiencing pain (e.g., when you are sick):
   a. Our pride decreases and we become more humble, appreciative, and receptive to others.
   b. We see the unsatisfactory nature of cyclic existence more clearly. This helps us to generate the determination to be free from cyclic existence and to attain liberation.
   c. Our compassion for others who are in pain increases because we understand their experience.
3. Do the taking and giving meditation.
4. Worldly people voluntarily endure many difficulties for worldly gain and reputation. Why can't we endure the difficulties and inconveniences involved in practicing Dharma, which will bring us ultimate peace and happiness?
5. If we train to be patient with small sufferings, then by the power of familiarity, we will later be able to endure big sufferings easily.

Jealousy

What is jealousy?

Jealousy is a mental factor that, out of attachment to respect and material gain, is unable to bear the good things that others have.

Joy is a mental state in which we rejoice when others have good qualities, opportunities, talents, material possessions, respect, love, and so on.

What are the disadvantages of jealousy?

1. We are unhappy and in turmoil and may not be able to sleep well.
2. Our own good qualities are exhausted.

3. We become fearful because someone else may get what we want.
4. Jealousy destroys cherished friendships.
5. It makes us look foolish in the eyes of those we respect.
6. Under its influence, we plot how to destroy others' happiness and, in the process, lose our own self-respect.
7. We slander, gossip, and speak badly of others.
8. We harm others and hurt their feelings.
9. We create negative karma, bringing more problems in future lives.
10. Jealousy destroys our virtue, thereby preventing us from receiving worldly and Dharma happiness.

What are its antidotes?

1. Remember the disadvantages of jealousy and the advantages of abandoning it. Jealousy only harms us.
2. Rejoice at the good fortune and qualities of others. By doing so, our mind becomes happy and we create great positive potential.
3. If the things we are jealous about are worldly objects (money, possessions, beauty, worldly knowledge, power, reputation, strength, talents, etc.), remember they bring us no ultimate happiness anyway. If they are Dharma qualities and virtues in others, remember that by others having them, we will benefit because these people will help us and all others.
4. Recall that we often say, "How wonderful it would be if others had happiness. I will work for the benefit of others." Now someone else is happy and we didn't even have to lift a finger to bring it about. So why begrudge him this happiness? This is especially true if it is only temporary, worldly happiness.
5. Jealousy does not give us what we desire. For example, whether our rival gets some money or not, it does not change the fact that we do not have it.
6. If we were the best and most talented, the world would be in sad shape because we are ignorant of so many things. Thus, it's good that others are more knowledgeable and capable than we are because we can benefit from what they do and can learn from them.

Pride and Arrogance

What is pride?

Pride is a mental factor that grasps strongly at the wrong conception of "I" and "mine" and inflates their importance, making us feel superior to others. We become puffed up and conceited.

Self-confidence and humility are mental states in which the mind is relaxed, receptive to learning, confident in our abilities, and content with our situation. We no longer feel the stress of needing to prove ourselves or to be recognized.

What are the disadvantages of pride?

1. We are condescending to those inferior to us, competitive with those of equal ability, and jealous of those who are better.
2. We look ridiculous and pathetic by showing off and bragging about ourselves.
3. Our mind is filled with stress from trying to prove ourselves.
4. We are easily offended.
5. Pride prevents us from learning and therefore is a big hindrance to spiritual progress.
6. We create negative karma that results in lower rebirth. Even when we are again reborn human, we will be poor, devoid of happiness, born in a lowly position, and have a bad reputation.

What are the antidotes to pride and arrogance?

1. Remember its disadvantages and the advantages of abandoning it.
2. All of our good qualities, wealth, talent, physical beauty, strength, and so forth come due to the kindness of others. If others did not give us this body, if they did not teach us, give us a job, and so forth, we would have nothing and would lack knowledge and good qualities. How can we think of ourselves as superior when none of these things originated solely from us?
3. Think about the twelve links, the twelve sources, eighteen constituents, and other difficult subjects. We will quickly see that we do not know much at all.

4. Remember our faults.
5. Recognize that arrogance is a thinly disguised, but ineffective, way to feel good about ourselves. Focus instead on developing genuine self-confidence based on having Buddha potential.
6. As long as we are still under the control of afflictions and karma and are obliged to take rebirth uncontrollably, what is there to be proud of?
7. The independent "I" that is grasped at as being so important does not exist at all.
8. Contemplate the good qualities of others, especially the Buddhas and bodhisattvas. We quickly see our qualities pale in comparison. It is more suitable for us to work hard to cultivate good qualities and to aspire to become like the Buddhas and bodhisattvas.
9. Confess our destructive actions. What is there to be proud of when we have so many negative karmic seeds on our mindstream?
10. Do prostrations in order to lessen our pride and to develop respect for those with good qualities.

15. Advice for Newcomers to the Dharma

I REMEMBER WELL my initial years in the Dharma, trying to figure out how to act in Dharma centers, in monasteries, and with monastics. Understanding what to study and practice was no easier. And learning to work with my mind was the greatest challenge of all! Some tips for those of you who are newcomers may help to ease your way.

When you go to a Dharma center, talk to the person in the reception area, ask if there is a brochure on etiquette, and borrow a prayer book or whatever handouts are available to use during the class. If there's no one greeting people at the door, ask someone who seems to know their way around the center. People are usually friendly. During Q&A time, ask questions. No question is "stupid." In fact, chances are that several other people in the room are wondering the same thing as you are and hope that someone will overcome their shyness enough to ask the teacher.

You will see people bowing. If you don't feel comfortable doing that, remain standing until they have finished and then sit down. Similarly, if the group does recitations before and after teachings or meditation, recite them if you feel comfortable, but simply remain silent if you do not. Do not pressure yourself to do anything you are unfamiliar with or do not understand. Instead, ask questions and think about the answers until you feel comfortable joining in with the bowing or chanting.

As a beginner, go to the classes for beginners. Although the center may be hosting initiations by well-known teachers, wait to attend those until you have established a proper foundation in the gradual path and in the thought transformation practices. Learn how to calm your mind and work with your afflictive emotions before delving into more complex practices. If you skip around from one class to another or frequently miss classes, you will miss learning important steps to practice. The importance of properly understanding basic Buddhist principles and establishing a solid foundation at the beginning cannot be overemphasized.

During Dharma teachings, you will hear many new ideas, some of which may not initially make sense to you. Buddhist practice is based on understanding, not blind faith, so do not try to force yourself to believe them. However, do not discard them as ridiculous either. Instead, put them on "the back burner" and return to contemplate them from time to time. Gradually they will begin to make sense.

Don't expect to understand or actualize everything all at once. It takes years, lifetimes, eons. Learning Dharma is not like Western education, where we learn facts and tell the teacher what they already know on a test. Learning Dharma is about transforming our mind and heart. So listen attentively to the Dharma when you are at a center, temple, or monastery. At home, spend time thinking about what you have heard. Check out the teachings by analyzing them with logic. Apply them to your life to see if they work. Listen to the teachings on the same topic many times; each time you hear it, it will sound different because your mind has changed. Read Dharma books slowly, pausing to contemplate what you have read and to apply it to your life. Although it's tempting to read hurriedly in order to get a lot of information—and especially to fulfill our curiosity about exotic practices—principally read books that correspond with your level of practice. In this way, you will establish a good foundation and will avoid confusion.

Buddhism is not intellectual concepts. Practice is essential to bring the Dharma into your heart. This entails setting up a regular daily meditation practice and sticking to it. Only by making meditation a part of your daily life routine will you experience its benefits. Refer to the chapter "Establishing a Daily Practice" to learn how to do this.

In your daily meditation practice, begin with reciting some verses to establish your motivation and make your mind receptive. Then do checking (analytical) meditation on the topics you learned in Dharma class. This formal time of meditation prepares you for practicing the Dharma the rest of your day—at work, with your family, at school, wherever. In those situations, be aware of what you're thinking, feeling, saying, and doing. Be mindful of your bodhicitta motivation and try to bring love and compassion into all your interactions with others. In the evening, review your day, congratulate yourself for what you did well, admit and regret any harmful actions, and renew your compassion so that you will greet the next day with joy.

When you first begin to practice, you may be startled at the thoughts and feelings you discover inside yourself. You may discover anger, jealousy, attachment, or pride that you didn't know was there. Don't get discouraged, by thinking the path is too difficult or by thinking you are incapable of actualizing it. All of us are similar; anyone who has practiced Dharma for a while has gone through what you are experiencing and has come out the other end. Be patient and gentle with yourself. Let go of unrealistic expectations.

Stay focused on what is important and don't get lost in the trappings. Dharma is about transforming our minds. Tibetan Buddhism has many fascinating external effects—high thrones, deep chanting, colorful brocade, and elaborate pujas. These are aids to practice. Actual practice is about working with our mind and heart.

There's no rush to find a teacher. Buddhist scriptures instruct us to check out someone's qualities well before entering into a mentor-disciple relationship. In the meantime, continue attending Dharma class and practice what you learn. Go slowly: take refuge and precepts and form a teacher-student relationship when you are ready. Sometimes an emotional feeling may suddenly surge up that makes you want to do this, but it's wiser to wait a while until your understanding is stable.

Cultivate friendships with people who are also practicing the Dharma. In this way, you will encourage each other to learn and practice. One way to meet people is to volunteer at the Dharma center. Start with a small job and do it well. Your Dharma practice is most important, so don't take on more volunteer work than you are able to handle.

We receive what we put into the Dharma. Our joyous effort brings good results over time. We are responsible for our spiritual practice, although we certainly depend on spiritual teachers to instruct us and a community of Dharma friends for support. However, no one is going to spoon-feed us. Our teachers and the Three Jewels are there to guide, teach, and inspire us, but we have to do the work of transforming our minds. As we do, we will become wiser, calmer, and more compassionate. Our mental and emotional clarity will increase, as will our sense of well-being.

16. Deepening Your Dharma Practice

Establishing a daily meditation practice is one part of our spiritual life. There are many other elements to it as well: studying under the guidance of a qualified teacher, engaging in the teachings, taking refuge and precepts, doing the preliminary practices (*ngondro*), transforming our daily life activities into the path, and understanding the role of ritual are among them. Let's look at these more closely to see how to use them to deepen our Dharma practice.

How to Engage the Teachings and the Teachers

Our practice progresses by developing the three types of wisdom: the wisdom arising from hearing, from thinking (reflecting), and from meditation. The first, the wisdom arising from hearing the teachings can also refer to studying or reading them. In ancient times literacy was not as widespread and books were not readily available, so most learning of the Dharma was done by listening to teachings. We study the teachings so that we will learn how to practice properly. Practicing includes more than meditation; it involves a way of life that includes training our body, speech, and mind. Practice involves how we relate to other people, how we speak, what we feel, and so forth. It touches every aspect of our life.

After hearing and studying the teachings, we must reflect on their meaning and develop the wisdom arising from thinking. In addition to reflection on the teachings while we're alone, discussing what we have heard with friends is important. For this reason, Tibetan monastics—and the Indian monastics before them—debate the teachings as part of developing the wisdom arising from thinking. Through discussion and reflection on the Dharma we refine our conceptual understanding of the Buddha's teachings, which is an essential preliminary in order to be able to practice them correctly.

Sometimes we may listen to a teaching and think we have understood it. However, only when we discuss it with our friends do we realize that our understanding is not as complete or as accurate as we had previously believed. When our friend asks us a question that we cannot answer, we should say, "Thank you for helping me to refine my understanding. I will study more and ask my teachers to clarify these points for me." Having consulted our teachers and Dharma friends, we then reflect more on what we have learned to ensure we understand the teachings properly.

When our conceptual understanding is correct, we then familiarize ourselves with the teachings by meditating on them. The wisdom arising from meditation is actually quite astute: it comes from a union of serenity and special insight, and thus is quite a high realization. The meditation we do as beginners is a preparation for that; during this time we train in stabilizing and analytical meditation.

From one perspective studying, thinking, and meditating are sequential. We have to study the teachings in order to reflect on them, and we have to reflect on them before we can familiarize ourselves with them through meditation. However, this does not mean that we must learn everything about a particular topic before we can reflect on it. Nor does it mean that we must reflect completely on a topic before engaging in any meditation. Rather, we can do all three during the course of a day. We learn a little, reflect on what we learned, meditate, and put it into practice. We do this while we continue to study and listen to more teachings and discuss the Dharma with friends.

This process of engaging with the teachings through hearing, reflecting, and meditating leads into the topic of cultivating a healthy and suitable relationship with a spiritual teacher. In order to learn the Dharma deeply, studying and practicing under the guidance of one or more wise and compassionate teachers is essential. While a book will give us information, studying with a living spiritual mentor bestows something much greater. A living person embodies the Dharma for us; his or her life is an example of how to study, reflect, meditate, and practice. Attending oral teachings, we may ask our questions and clarify particular points with our spiritual mentor. Meeting with our teacher at other times, we may request personal guidance in our practice. Serving our teachers directly, we learn by observing how they handle various situations. By assisting them in their projects that benefit others, we have the opportunity to serve sentient beings and to repay our teachers' kindness.

In short, something happens when we're with living practitioners that doesn't happen when we're reading a book. Some of this may be challenging to our egos, but if we are sincere in our practice, this is a boon. A book does not notice our faults and point them out to us. Our spiritual teacher may. We can pick up a book and read it anytime we want and put it down when we are tired. However, we must readjust our schedule and preferences to accord with the teaching times and venues of our spiritual mentors.

Having heard the benefits of having a spiritual teacher, some people become eager to form that kind of relationship with the first person who comes along. This is not wise. Not everyone who is called a teacher is necessarily a qualified teacher, and even among qualified spiritual mentors, we have to form the mentor-trainee relationship with those that truly speak to our heart and whom we deeply trust. This is not a relationship to rush into or to treat in a nonchalant manner.

As a beginner, start by reading books and attending teachings by various people. Go to different Buddhist centers, get to know the teachers, listen to the teachings, observe which teachers you feel a connection with, and which practices you find helpful. Check the teachers' qualities: Do they live ethically and keep whatever precepts they have undertaken? Are they compassionate to everyone? Do they have a good relationship with their own teachers? Have they studied and practiced for a long time? Are they humble and not possessive of disciples? Do they have a broad depth of understanding or do they focus only on one practice? Is what they teach in accord with general Buddhist principles and teachings?

For some people, finding a teacher in whom they feel confidence takes more time than for others. A mentor-disciple relationship is not something to rush into. Take as long as you need to find a qualified spiritual teacher and a Buddhist tradition that fits you. At the beginning you may not have a teacher. That's okay. You can learn the teachings, put them into practice, and start a daily practice without having a teacher—other than Shakyamuni Buddha, who, His Holiness the Dalai Lama continuously reminds us, is our Teacher. Slowly, as you become more involved in the Dharma and ascertain its value in your life, then forming a relationship with a qualified teacher is important.

Because of my website, www.thubtenchodron.org, which contains many audio and written teachings, some people who have never met me and who have never been to a Dharma center write to ask if I will be their teacher. This is a difficult situation because on one hand, I want to help these people. On the other hand, it is better for them if they receive oral teachings directly from a teacher. It is difficult to develop a mentor-disciple relationship via the Internet, not only because the personal connection is not there, but also because such a relationship requires time and attention that is not possible online. So I usually respond that I will help them as much as I am able to, and recommend that, in addition, they attend a retreat I am leading or go to a local Dharma center.

Sometimes the spiritual mentor with whom you resonate doesn't live near you. That means you have to put in the effort to travel to where he or she is teaching. Some people say, "It's so far. I don't have the money. I don't have the time. Why can't my teacher come here?" While on one level, thinking in this way may seem perfectly valid, on another, I believe it is indicative of our consumer mentality. There may be the subtle assumption, "I'm the customer, and you're marketing something. You should come to me and convince me that I should get your product." However, a relationship with a spiritual mentor is not a consumer relationship. It cannot thrive with that mentality. Such a way of thinking, however obvious or subtle, hinders an actual spiritual relationship. When we read the biographies of the great masters, we see that they gave up whatever conveniences were necessary in order to receive teachings because they valued the teachings beyond all else. Because they cherished the Dharma so much, they benefited from hearing it, and with joyous effort they put it into practice. If we lack such sincerity, even if our teachers came to teach us, we wouldn't derive the same benefit.

When I met the Dharma in 1975 it was very difficult to find teachers in the West. I quit my job, took the little savings I had, and literally went halfway around the world to Nepal and India to study with Tibetan masters because I felt the Dharma was valuable in my life. So when people who have a job tell me the half-hour drive across town to get to the Dharma center is too long or that they don't have enough money to cover the room and board at retreat centers, it's hard for me to sympathize. Some people think that their teachers should sit on airplanes for hours on end and suffer jetlag after crossing many time zones in order to come to teach them, the students. But such an attitude towards our mentors is not conducive for spiritual advancement. Our relationships with our spiritual mentors are the most important relationships we have because these people lead us to fulfill our highest aspiration, enlightenment. Therefore, treating our teachers with respect and consideration is worthy of our attention.

When you have to put your energy into something, you value it. When you listen to a profound teaching on the Internet, while sitting in your favorite reclining chair, eating potato chips and drinking a Coke, something is missing! When you have to spend a half hour driving to the teaching site or fly to where your teacher is offering a retreat or take time off of work to be able to go to teachings, you will value the teachings you hear. The process of giving up some of your comfort or pleasure indicates that the Dharma is important to you and that, as a result, you will pay attention to the teachings and absorb what you hear.

It's said that every step you take to get to a place where the Dharma is being taught creates positive potential because your intention is to learn the Dharma, improve the state of your mind, and progress on the path to liberation and enlightenment. Your traveling to your spiritual mentor is part of your Dharma practice and your mind is joyous even if there are difficulties along the way. If thoughts arise, such as, "My teacher should make it easier. This practice session is too long; I want it to end sooner," "It's not convenient when the teachings start at 7:30. I want them to start at 7:00," or "My teacher should tell more jokes and be more entertaining," you recognize them as complaining mind, not Dharma mind, and let them go.

Treasuring our Dharma guides is important. Just having the opportunity to meet a qualified teacher means we accumulated a lot of positive potential in previous lives. Let's respect the effort we made in previous lives that enables us to encounter the teachings and a qualified teacher now and cherish the opportunity. Let's respect our teachers and serve them. We offer service to our Dharma teachers because they are working for the benefit of all sentient beings and we want to contribute to such wonderful endeavors.

DEVELOPING YOUR PRACTICE FURTHER

As your practice deepens, your trust in the Buddhas, Dharma, and Sangha naturally increases. This happens because you have listened to teachings, examined them, and found that they are logically consistent. In addition, you have put the teachings into practice and discovered that they help you. As a result, you now are confident that Buddhism is the spiritual path you want to follow, and you would like to affirm that in a ceremony. At this point, you may request your spiritual mentor to conduct the ceremony of taking refuge in the Three Jewels. During this brief ceremony you repeat the Three Refuges after your spiritual mentor. At this time, you may also choose to take some or all of the five lay precepts: to avoid killing, stealing, unwise sexual behavior, lying, and taking intoxicants. Taking refuge and precepts in this way helps to make your commitment to your spiritual path firm.

Another way to enhance your practice is by doing retreat each year. Retreat is a period of time—anywhere from a few days to many months or even years—when we restrict other activities and disengage from the hurry and flurry of our lives in order to focus on meditation. During this time, we do several meditation sessions a day. Group retreats are particularly popular because keeping the meditation schedule is easier when the people around you are doing the same thing. Many retreat centers have retreats that you can attend. The schedule, discipline, and practice you do during a retreat differ depending on the teacher who is leading it. Sometimes what is called a "retreat" nowadays is more like a course in which there are periods of teachings, discussion or Q&A, and meditation. These are very beneficial, because you have the opportunity to go deeper into your practice with fewer distractions.

Participating in a day-long retreat at a Dharma center will also refresh your mind and rejuvenate your practice. If you have had the transmission for the Eight Mahayana Precepts ceremony, you can take them on your own for a day. During that day, you take special care to abandon 1) killing, 2) stealing, 3) sexual activity, 4) lying, and 5) taking intoxicants. In addition, you avoid 6) singing, dancing, and playing music; 7) wearing cosmetics and ornaments, and sitting on high or luxurious seats or beds; and 8) eating at improper times, that is, you eat only one meal and finish eating by midday. The meal must be vegetarian. Some teachers, however, permit eating breakfast and lunch, as long as no solid food is eaten after midday. Keeping precepts for one day like this will increase your mindfulness and turn your mind towards the Dharma.

As you become more involved in the Dharma and see the benefits of practice, your priorities may change and you may want to attend a longer retreat. At that point, attend a week or two weeks of group retreat. As your practice advances more, you may want to go on a month or even a three-month retreat. Many people find these longer group retreats helpful for deepening their practice. At Sravasti Abbey, we do a three-month group retreat each winter. During this time, we keep silence, except for a weekly teaching and a bi-monthly community meeting. If you are self-disciplined, have received all necessary instructions, and understand how to do the practice, doing a solitary retreat is fine. If you do that, it's wise to have a teacher or other meditators in the area with whom you can consult.

Westerners tend to be idealistic about retreat. We hear stories of the great meditators such as Milarepa and then think we will go on a long retreat in a cave. While having such aspirations is, of course, virtuous, we have to check to see if we are currently capable of doing a long, solitary retreat. It sounds good, until we go to an isolated place and then find we're spending a lot of time missing our friends, craving ice cream, and daydreaming about how much others will admire and respect us when our retreat is finished! It is more practical to go one step at a time and build a good foundation. Similar to constructing a house: building a solid foundation never goes to waste and a long-lasting, stable structure can be built on it. But if we rush and pour a shoddy foundation, we will have continuous problems no matter what we construct on top of it. Being a simple practitioner, with noble aspirations and a humble and practical approach, is best.

As your practice develops, at some point you may want to begin some of the preliminary practices. These practices are done especially to purify negative karma and to accumulate positive potential. Our mind is like a field, and purifying and accumulating positive potential are comparable to tilling and fertilizing it. If a field is well prepared, when seeds are planted and the weather is conducive, crops will naturally grow. Similarly, when our mind is free from gross negative karmic seeds and enriched with positive potential, then when we listen to teachings and put them into practice, understanding will come and our mind will be transformed.

The number and method of doing the ngondro practices differ depending on the tradition. There may be four, five, or nine preliminary practices. The expanded version consists of nine ngondro practices: 1) prostrations, 2) mandala offering, 3) taking refuge, 4) Vajrasattva mantra, 5) guru yoga, 6) Dorje Khandro (Vajradaka) fire offering, 7) Damtsig Dorje (Samaya Vajra) mantra, 8) water bowls, and 9) tsa-tsa, the small clay images. Some traditions complete the preliminary practices by doing one at a time, others do a little of each every day. Some teachers encourage their students to do them in a retreat setting, others as a daily practice.

Usually one hundred thousand repetitions of a practice are done, but added to this is another 10% to accommodate for errors, so the actual number is 111,111. The number is not, however, so important, and we should not be distracted by counting while doing the practices. Rather, the process and mental transformation that occur are to be emphasized.

These practices are not mandatory but they are recommended. However, since some of them involve rituals that you may initially not understand or be inclined to do, it's best to gain a firm footing in the gradual path meditations before embarking on the ngondro. Even when doing ngondro, continue with the gradual path meditations. As His Holiness the Dalai Lama mentioned in his endorsement, "As I often tell people, the analytical meditations on the points of the lamrim will transform our minds and enable us to become more compassionate and wise. I encourage people to do these meditations as part of their daily practice."

DHARMA FRIENDS

Having Dharma friends is a real boost to your practice because we are influenced by the people with whom we associate. Dharma friends not only encourage us to practice, but also understand a part of us that other people may not understand or be interested in. You can be open with your Dharma friends because they understand the various issues that may arise in Dharma practice. They are able to share their experiences and offer assistance. For example, if you're having a problem waking up in the morning in order to meditate, chances are some of your Dharma friends have encountered this as well. Sometimes we feel as if we're the only ones having a certain difficulty, but when we share this with our Dharma friends, we discover that they have had to deal with this as well. They can then share their experiences and solutions in a supportive way.

Cultivating friendships with the people at the Dharma center that we attend enables us to build a community of like-minded people. Many of us want to be part of a community, but we don't always know how to do it. So instead of rushing off after teachings or group meditation, stay and talk to the other people at the center. If you have time, volunteer to help with activities. This is an excellent way to meet people. In addition, by offering help, we learn many things about the Dharma.

As you make friends with Dharma people, you will talk about a variety of topics, but try to focus most of your conversations on the Dharma. At the Dharma center, don't chit-chat about movies or other insignificant topics with your Dharma friends. Really treasure your Dharma friends and talk with them about things that are important to you. Group discussions, which are preceded by a meditation on a particular topic, are a wonderful way to share. People learn to open up and trust each other because they are talking about topics that relate to their lives and their Dharma practice. For example, you may want to discuss visualization meditations and how they have affected your practice. Or you might talk about rebirth, forgiving and apologizing, and other topics related to integrating the teachings in your life. When discussing these topics with Dharma friends, everyone opens up and shares their perspective, not from an intellectual point of view, but from a personal one. This results in wonderful conversations that boost our practice and develop meaningful friendships.

TRANSFORMING DAILY LIFE ACTIONS INTO THE PATH

Meditation sessions give us periods of quiet, undisturbed time to contemplate Dharma points in depth. A sitting practice is preparation for responding to daily life situations from a Dharma perspective. By applying the teachings to our interactions with other people and the emotions and attitudes that arise during the day, we learn to transform ordinary actions into the path. For example, most of us spend some time cleaning during the day. Instead of viewing this as a chore that we heedlessly rush through with the goal of finishing it as soon as possible, we can transform it into an action that creates positive potential by thinking in a different way. For example, when doing your dishes, we think that the soap and water represent the wisdom realizing emptiness and we are cleaning the defilements from our own and other sentient beings' minds as we wash the plates. This becomes an opportunity to cultivate bodhicitta as well as a time to contemplate the wisdom realizing emptiness.

Similarly, when you're vacuuming, imagine taking all sentient beings' sufferings away from them, thus freeing them from the three types of dukkha. When you go down stairs, think, "I'm willing to go to the lower realms to be of benefit to sentient beings." When you walk up stairs, think, "I'm leading all sentient beings to enlightenment." Changing diapers is another activity of cleaning, in which you may think, "May I cleanse the suffering and causes of suffering from the minds of all sentient beings." Or you may reflect, "My parents cleaned my diapers. All sentient beings have been my parents in previous lives; they took care of me with love and care when I was an infant." With increased gratitude, you will recognize others' kindness that you may previously have taken for granted.

Before going to work each morning, generate a good motivation, thinking, "I'm going to offer service. Whomever I come in contact with today, be they colleagues, clients, or others, I want to benefit them in whatever big or small way possible." Enlarge your motivation for going to work: instead of simply seeking to support yourself and your family, have the intention not to harm and to be of benefit to everyone you meet that day. If you have difficulty remembering to pause and generate this motivation, put a post-it on your fridge, on your bag, or on the steering wheel. Deliberately cultivating this motivation will transform your day.

So many people live their lives on automatic, barely conscious of what they are doing or why they are doing it. For example, you get in the car, turn the key, put the radio on, and drive away. But where are you going? And for what purpose? When you arrive at your destination, if someone asked you what you thought about during the trip, you might have difficulty answering because both the car and your mind were on cruise control. So, when you get in the car, sit quietly for a moment and ask yourself, "Where am I going? Why am I going there?" If you have a distinct destination and clear purpose, then make the trip. If not, welcome the free time you've discovered. Instead of running one errand each day, which consumes a lot of time and gasoline, arrange your life so that you do several errands on one trip and have time left over for your spiritual practice.

Use the time you spend traveling to put the Dharma into practice. For example, instead of listening to the radio when you're in the car, listen to a Dharma tape or chant mantras. When you are caught in a traffic jam look around at the people in the other cars and remember, "These sentient beings have been kind to me in previous lives and are being kind to me now." Instead of eagerly awaiting the chance to cut someone off and drive ahead, think, "These people want to be happy just like me. They want to be free of suffering just like me." Focus on that and let your heart open towards them. When you're in line at the grocery store, reflect, "So many sentient beings grew this food, harvested, transported, and packaged it. They put it on the shelves so that I can buy it. I depend upon these people whom I don't even know and yet who make it possible for me to have food. How kind they are to do their jobs!" In this way, feel connected to the people around you. That might lead you to thank the employees. How wonderful they would feel if you did!

I travel a lot and make it a point to thank the people who clean the airport bathrooms. I thank the garbage collector, the people laying telephone wire, and those doing road construction. Our lives are dependent upon them and yet we take them for granted and seldom think to thank them. When we use everyday experiences to realize our dependence on others' kindness, the way we act and the way we relate to the people around us changes. We begin to share a smile or some kind words with them, and when we do, all of us feel good.

Sustaining Your Dharma Practice

People often ask me, "What gives you the energy to keep going in your practice?" The key is motivation, specifically the loving, compassionate attitude of bodhicitta.

Many people initially come to the Dharma because they are going through a tough time. They are seeking a way to end their immediate unhappiness. They learn a little Dharma—for example, how to work with anger—and practicing it, they feel better. They are satisfied and stop meditating and attending Dharma teachings. To continue practicing beyond that point requires expanding the motivation from wanting to end immediate suffering to something more long-term, that is, a motivation seeking a good rebirth, aspiring for liberation from cyclic existence, or wishing to become a Buddha for the benefit of sentient beings.

Such motivations depend on understanding the Buddhist worldview as described in the Four Noble Truths. This view may seem foreign to those of us who grew up thinking that only what we experience with our senses exists. However, while we consider ourselves empirical and scientific, in fact we often accept things on faith. For example, most of us accept the latest scientific discoveries even though we didn't do the experiment or analyze the data. Even when scientists revise their understandings, dismissing as erroneous previous discoveries, we continue to trust their research. Do we trust the Buddha's teachings in a similar way?

One way to develop confidence in the Buddha's teachings is to think about them and see if they describe your experiences and observations in life. Another way is to practice according to the teachings and see the results that ensue. If your mind becomes calmer and your heart kinder, you will know from your own experience that the teachings work. For example, if you apply the Buddha's teachings on how to forgive and let go of a grudge, and find that they help you to do just that, automatically you will have confidence in the Buddha as a reliable spiritual guide. Based on this experience, you may trust what he taught regarding other topics that you cannot readily ascertain for yourself. This is very different from blind faith.

Looking at the lives of wise practitioners can also stimulate our faith in the efficacy of the Buddha's teachings and encourage us to practice. Reading the biographies of practitioners in India and Tibet will inspire us to practice with similar diligence and consistency. The lives of contemporary Asian and Western practitioners—how they live and how they use the Dharma to handle a variety of situations—provide a good example for us. Look at how older students have changed due to their practice.

When doing this, however, it's important to avoid idolizing people or expecting them to be perfect. A new student once commented about the behavior of a senior student to another practitioner, saying, "She's been practicing Dharma for so many years, but is still so irascible and difficult to get along with. Does the Dharma really work?" To this the other practitioner replied, "You should have known her before she began practicing the Dharma. She was even more difficult then! The Dharma has really helped her."

Discipline is important in order to sustain our practice. When it comes to earning money we are extremely disciplined. We don't mind working diligently or enduring hardships in order to get what our mind of attachment craves. Working overtime to earn more money, taking on more work to get a promotion, finding a way to be nice to someone we don't like in order to close a business deal—we will do these without hesitation to get what we want.

We need to have similar patience, energy, and perseverance in our meditation practice, knowing that it, too, will lead us to our goals, even if some of the results of our spiritual endeavors may not manifest until future lives. While our worldly efforts are not always successful, our spiritual ones eventually will be. Any and all constructive karma we create will bear fruit. When we create the causes for Dharma realizations, they will occur because of the law of causality.

While being firm with our wandering attention is necessary at the beginning, once we begin to experience the benefits of consistent Dharma practice, continuing with it will be easier. After a while practice becomes part of our daily life and as essential to our well-being as eating. Thus we practice everyday because we know it nourishes us. At that time, attending Dharma classes and retreats will be high on our priority list, and without an internal struggle, we will be sure to do them.

The Role of Ritual

Some people question the role of ritual in Buddhist practice. They think that the Buddha just taught meditation and encouraged people to relate to the "here and now" free from the fabrications of ritual.

In fact, the Buddha taught an entire way of life, as encompassed in the Eightfold Noble Path: correct view, intention, speech, action, livelihood, effort, mindfulness, and concentration. This way of life includes learning the teachings, reflecting on them, and meditating on them, as discussed earlier. It involves trying to live them in our daily lives.

All of us have rituals that we perform on a daily basis. For example, most people have "rituals" that they do each morning when they get up. Having a cup of coffee and reading the newspaper is a ritual for some people. Brushing our teeth in a particular way is a ritual each one of us has developed. Our ways of greeting each other in different contexts are rituals. There are rituals that mark transitions in life: birth, the first day of school, birthdays, graduation, marriage, and death. Rituals provide structure and stability in our lives. In other words, ritual is not foreign to us, no matter how secular our life is.

In spiritual practice, the purpose of ritual is to transform our mind. Rituals are not done for their own sake; that would be meaningless. An example of a ritual is the "Meditation on the Buddha." Here we imagine the Buddha, take refuge in the Three Jewels, generate bodhicitta, contemplate the four immeasurables, the seven-limb prayer, and so on. Paying attention to each step of this ritual enables us to absorb its meaning, and in this way our mind is transformed through generating the positive attitudes and emotions that the recitations and visualizations evoke in us. If we just recite a ritual without contemplating its meaning or while distracted by other objects, the effects are minimal because our mind is not transformed. But if we focus on what we are doing, change occurs. For example, when meditating on the Buddha, we spend a few minutes feeling that we are in the presence of an enlight-ened one. We imagine being surrounded by all living beings (actually we are always surrounded by all living beings; this visualization is simply reminding us of this fact). Contemplating the disadvantages of cyclic existence, from our hearts we turn to the Three Jewels for spiritual guidance because we wish to alleviate the pain of all beings—ourselves and others—and increase our genuine happiness. At this point, when we do the recitation of taking refuge in the Buddha, Dharma, and Sangha, the words come from our heart and our mind is transformed. Similarly, the actions of making prostrations and offerings every morning transform our minds. We become more receptive, respectful, generous, and joyful.

All Buddhist traditions use rituals such as bowing, making offerings, revealing and regretting our mistaken actions, and dedicating the positive potential from our actions. All use rituals for contemplation before eating, for offering monastics the four requisites—food, clothing, shelter, and medicine—and for greeting our spiri-tual mentors. All have rituals for lay practitioners to take refuge in the Three Jewels and receive the lay precepts, and for new monastics to be admitted into the Order.

I have noticed that when we do a particular ritual for a long time, it ceases to feel like a "made up" activity, but instead becomes "the way things are done." Then, when we visit a group with different patterns of behavior, we think, "They do a lot of rit-ual." That thought arises simply because we are still unfamiliar with their rituals and feel somewhat awkward doing them. However, as we become more familiar with them, they cease to appear to be rituals to us and instead we relate to them as nor-mal occurrences.

The meditations on a Buddha figure are guided meditations, designed to train and direct our minds in a constructive direction. Some people find these meditations effective because the steps of the ritual enable them to focus better and be less distracted. The structure of the ritual guides them so they know what to contemplate and in what order. Other people do not like rituals very much. They may prefer to go through the same steps, but to express the meaning of the reflections in their own words rather than repeating written verses. Some people prefer to do silent meditation without chanting aloud. Others are more attracted to analytical meditation on the lamrim and not visualizations or mantra recitation.

We are free to choose how to apportion our time among the various practices. Each individual will decide this differently because various meditation practices will speak to the heart of one individual more than to another. Structure your practice in a way that helps you, realizing that this may change over time. In doing this, however, make sure that you do the practices in the way the Buddha and your spiritual mentors instruct. Avoid creating your own practices; we are not enlightened beings and doing practices that we make up will be distracting at the least and disastrous at the worst.

As we continue to learn the Dharma and follow the path, questions will arise in your minds. When they do, it is wise to turn to your spiritual teachers. Do not think, "I'm the only one who has ever had this doubt, problem, or experience." Our Dharma friends may be working with similar issues and they can provide helpful perspectives. Also, many practitioners who have worked their way through these situations have preceded us and we can rely on their guidance. Be confident that resources are always available when we look for them.

Appendix 1. Contents of Guided Meditations on the CD

A1. Introduction (6:44)
A2. Meditation on the Buddha (37:42)
A3. Breathing Meditation (17:21)
A4. Recitations (6:15)
A5. Dedication (2:46)

Introduction to the Buddhist View

B1. Mind is the Source of Happiness and Pain (10:33)
B2. Taking the Ache out of Attachment (16:07)
B3. Transforming Attachment (17:01)
B4. The Nature of Mind (14:34)
B5. Mind and Rebirth (15:38)
B6. The Four Noble Truths (17:22)
B7. The Three Characteristics (20:41)

The Path in Common with the Initial Level Practitioner

C1. Precious Human Life (16:56)
C2. The Purpose and Opportunity of a Precious Human Life (14:49)
C3. The Rarity and Difficulty of Attaining a Precious Human Life (20:22)
C4. The Eight Worldly Concerns (15:02)
D1. The Nine-Point Death Meditation (34:16)

THE PATH IN COMMON WITH THE MIDDLE LEVEL PRACTITIONER

THE PATH OF THE ADVANCED PRACTITIONER

G3. Far-Reaching Patience: The Disadvantages of Anger (14:33)

G4. Far-Reaching Patience: The Antidotes to Anger (19:10)

G5. Far-Reaching Joyous Effort (18:59)

G6. Far-Reaching Concentration (12:03)

G7. Far-Reaching Wisdom: Dependent Arising (14:56)

G8. Far-Reaching Wisdom: Emptiness (24:38)

G9. How to Rely on a Spiritual Mentor (30:01)

Please note: Some meditations which are on one track on the audio recording are divided into two or more meditations in the chapter "Lamrim Meditation Outlines."

Appendix 2. Full Outline for the Meditation on the Precious Human Life

The Eight Freedoms

Our present life is free from eight types of rebirth that would greatly hinder our ability to learn Dharma teachings, contemplate their meaning, and meditate on them. We are free from four nonhuman states, being born as a:

1. hell being
2. hungry ghost (*preta*)
3. animal
4. long-lived god

We are free from four human states, being born:

5. as a barbarian, among uncivilized savages, or in a country where religion is outlawed
6. where the Buddha's teachings are unavailable, i.e., in a world where the Buddha has not appeared
7. having physical or mental challenges that impede one's being able to learn and contemplate the Dharma
8. holding deeply entrenched distorted views

THE TEN FORTUNES

Our present life is also endowed with ten excellent factors which are conducive to being able to learn, practice, and realize the Buddha's teachings.

It is endowed with five personal factors:

1. birth as a human being
2. birth in a central Buddhist region (Geographically, this refers to our world; spiritually, it is where the fourfold Buddhist community exists—fully ordained male and female monastics and male and female lay followers who have taken refuge and precepts.)
3. having complete sense faculties, sound mental faculties, normal sex organs (not being a hermaphrodite or someone without sex organs)
4. not having committed the five heinous actions (killing one's father, mother, or an arhat; drawing blood from a Buddha; and causing a schism in the monastic sangha)
5. having instinctive belief in things worthy of respect such as the Three Jewels, ethical conduct, and so forth

It is endowed with five factors that come from society:

1. being born where and when a Buddha has appeared
2. being born where and when a Buddha has taught the Dharma
3. living where and when the Buddhadharma still exists (The scriptural Dharma exists where the Three Baskets of Buddha's teachings are propagated. The realized Dharma exists where people have the realizations gained from practice.)
4. living where and when there is a monastic sangha community following the Buddha's teachings
5. living where and when there are others with loving concern—Dharma teachers and benefactors—so that we have the external supports for practice

GLOSSARY

altar (shrine) A place reminding us of our spiritual potential and aspiration. A Buddhist altar may contain photos of our spiritual teachers, pictures or statues of the Buddha and tantric deities, Dharma texts, offerings, and so forth.

altruistic intention (Skt: *bodhicitta*) The mind dedicated to attaining enlightenment in order to benefit all sentient beings most effectively.

analytical meditation (checking meditation) Meditation that involves investigating a subject. It is done to develop insight into the nature of reality. It principally leads to special insight (Skt: *vipashyana*).

arhat A person who has attained liberation and is free from cyclic existence.

arya A person who has realized emptiness directly and is thus one of the Sangha Jewels of refuge.

bodhicitta *See* altruistic intention.

bodhisattva A person whose spontaneous reaction upon seeing any sentient being is "I aspire to become a Buddha in order to benefit them."

Buddha Any person who has purified all defilements and developed all good qualities. "The Buddha" refers to Shakyamuni Buddha, who lived 2,500 years ago in India.

Buddha nature (Buddha potential) The innate qualities of the mind enabling all beings to attain enlightenment.

Buddhahood *See* enlightenment.

calm abiding *See* serenity.

checking meditation *See* analytical meditation.

compassion The wish for sentient beings to be free from suffering and its causes.

concentration (Skt: *samadhi*) A mental factor that focuses single-pointedly on an object of meditation.

cyclic existence (Skt: *samsara*) Being uncontrollably reborn under the influence of mental afflictions and karmic latencies.

determination to be free (renunciation) The determination to be free from the sufferings of cyclic existence and to attain liberation.

Dharma The teachings of the Buddha. The Dharma Jewel is the third and fourth of the Four Noble Truths: the wisdom realizing emptiness and the cessation of suffering and its causes.

Dharma wheel An eight- or thousand-spoked wheel that symbolizes teaching the Dharma.

distorted views Stubborn and closed-minded views that the Three Jewels, cause and effect, and so on do not exist; believing that sentient beings are inherently selfish and cannot become enlightened.

disturbing attitudes and negative emotions (Skt: *klesha*) *See* mental afflictions.

dorje, double dorje (Skt: *vajra*) A tantric implement symbolizing the method aspect of the path. A double dorje is two dorjes perpendicular to each other and crossing at their centers. This symbolizes long life.

dukkha Any unsatisfactory condition, including physical and mental pain, fleeting worldly happiness, and having a body and mind under the influence of ignorance and karma.

emptiness (Skt: *shunyata*) The lack of independent or inherent existence, the ultimate nature or reality of all persons and phenomena.

enlightenment (Buddhahood) The state of a Buddha, i.e., the state of having forever eliminated all obscurations from the mindstream and having developed all good qualities and wisdom to their fullest extent. Buddhahood supersedes liberation.

field of positive potential The assembly of lineage masters, Buddhas, bodhisattvas, arhats, and so forth. We imagine this assembly and offer the seven-limb prayer in their presence in order to create positive potential (merit) that enriches our mindstream and enables us to develop spiritual realizations.

four immeasurables Equanimity, love, compassion, and joy.

glance meditation Briefly reflecting on the major steps of the path to enlightenment. Reciting a short text facilitates this.

gradual path to enlightenment (Tib: *lamrim*; stages of the path to enlightenment) A systematic, step-by-step presentation of the Buddha's teachings found in Tibetan Buddhism.

inherent or **independent existence** A false and nonexistent mode of being that we project onto persons and phenomena; existence independent of causes and conditions, parts, or the mind conceiving and labeling phenomena.

introspective alertness (vigilance, clear comprehension) A mental factor that is watchful so that we are aware of the contents of our mind. It enables us to bring our mind and actions back to ethical behavior or to the object of meditation if it has strayed.

karma Actions done by our body, speech, or mind.

karmic latency (karmic seed) The residual "energy" left on the mindstream when an action has been completed. When these latencies mature, they influence what we experience.

liberation (Skt: *moksha*) Freedom from cyclic existence.

love The wish for sentient beings to have happiness and its causes.

Mahayana A Buddhist tradition that emphasizes the development of the altruistic intention.

mandala The universe; the pure abode of a meditational deity. The mandala offering is done by imagining our world and everything beautiful in it and then offering this to the Buddhas and bodhisattvas.

mantra A series of Sanskrit syllables spoken by a Buddha that expresses the essence of the entire path to enlightenment. They are recited in order to concentrate and purify the mind.

meditation Habituating ourselves with positive attitudes and correct perspectives.

meditative quiescence *See* serenity.

mental afflictions Disturbing attitudes and negative emotions, such as ignorance, attachment, anger, pride, jealousy, and closed-mindedness, that disturb our mental peace and propel us to act in ways harmful to ourselves and others.

merit *See* positive potential.

mind The experiential, cognitive part of sentient beings; clarity and awareness. Formless, the mind isn't made of atoms, nor is it perceivable through our five senses.

mindfulness A mental factor that enables the mind to stay on its chosen object without forgetting it and prevents distraction to other objects.

mindstream Continuity of mind.

nirvana The cessation of dukkha and its causes; the emptiness of the mind in which dukkha and its causes have been ceased.

object of negation A way or mode of being that does not exist.

offerings Actual or imagined objects that we offer to the merit field in order to generate delight in giving and to create positive potential.

positive potential (merit) That which results in happiness in the future.

precepts Guidelines set out by the Buddha to help us refrain from destructive actions and to train our mind.

preliminary practices (Tib: *ngondro*) Practices done to purify negative karma and create positive potential, in preparation for a tantric retreat.

realization A clear, deep, and correct understanding of the conventional or ultimate natures. It may be either conceptual or nonconceptual, direct experience.

sadhana The method of meditating on the Buddha or a Buddha figure that is often written in the form of a text.

Sangha Any person who directly and nonconceptually realizes emptiness. In a more general sense, sangha refers to the communities of four or more fully-ordained monks or nuns.

selflessness The nonexistence of the object of negation.

sentient being Any being with a mind who is not a Buddha. This includes ordinary beings as well as arhats and bodhisattvas.

serenity (Skt: *shamatha*) The ability to remain single-pointedly on an object of meditation with a blissful and pliant mind for as long as one wishes. Also called "calm abiding" or "meditative quiescence."

seven-limb prayer A recitation in which we 1) bow, 2) make offerings, 3) reveal with regret our destructive actions, 4) rejoice in our own and others' virtue, 4) request the Buddhas to remain in our world, 6) request our teachers and the Buddhas to guide and teach us, and 7) dedicate our positive potential for the enlightenment of all sentient beings.

six far-reaching practices or attitudes (Skt: *paramita*) States of mind and practices cultivated with the bodhicitta motivation. The six far-reaching practices are generosity, ethical conduct, patience, joyous effort, meditative stabilization, and wisdom.

special insight (Skt: *vipashyana*; Pali: *vipassana*) Discriminating analytical wisdom. Special insight into emptiness realizes the empty nature of phenomena.

stabilizing meditation Meditation that stabilizes the mind by developing concentration. It leads principally to serenity.

suffering *See* dukkha.

sutra (Pali: *sutta*) A discourse given by the Buddha.

taking refuge Entrusting our spiritual development to the guidance of the Buddhas, Dharma, and Sangha.

tantra Literally, "thread" or "continuity." The texts of Vajrayana Buddhism; often used to refer to Vajrayana practice itself.

Three Higher Trainings Ethical conduct, concentration, and wisdom.

Three Jewels (Triple Gem) The Buddhas, Dharma, and Sangha.

three poisonous attitudes Ignorance, anger (hostility), and attachment. They poison our mind and motivate actions that poison our relationships.

three principal aspects of the path   The determination to be free, altruistic intention (bodhi-citta), and correct view.

unsatisfactory circumstances   *See* dukkha.

Vajradhara   The form in which Shakyamuni Buddha appeared to teach the Vajrayana.

Vajrayana   A Mahayana Buddhist tradition popular in Tibet and Japan.

wisdom realizing emptiness   A mind that correctly understands the manner in which all persons and phenomena exist, that is, the wisdom realizing the emptiness of inherent existence.

SUGGESTED READING

Berzin, Alexander. *Relating to a Spiritual Teacher: Building a Healthy Relationship.* Ithaca, N.Y.: Snow Lion Publications, 2000.

Chodron, Thubten. *Buddhism for Beginners.* Ithaca, N.Y.: Snow Lion Publications, 2001.

Chodron, Thubten. *Cultivating a Compassionate Heart: The Yoga Method of Chenrezig.* Ithaca, N.Y.: Snow Lion Publications, 2006.

Chodron, Thubten. *How to Free Your Mind: Tara the Liberator.* Ithaca, N.Y.: Snow Lion Publications, 2005.

Chodron, Thubten. *Open Heart, Clear Mind.* Ithaca, N.Y.: Snow Lion Publications, 1990.

Chodron, Thubten. *Taming the Mind.* Ithaca, N.Y.: Snow Lion Publications, 2004.

Chodron, Thubten. *Working with Anger.* Ithaca, N.Y.: Snow Lion Publications, 2001.

Deshung Rinpoche Kunga Tenpay Nyima. *The Three Levels of Spiritual Perception.* Translated by Jared Rhoton. Boston: Wisdom Publications, 1995.

Dhammananda, K. Sri. *How to Live Without Fear and Worry.* Kuala Lumpur: Buddhist Missionary Society, 1989.

Dhargyey, Geshe Ngawang. *An Anthology of Well-Spoken Advice.* Dharamsala, India: Library of Tibetan Works and Archives, 1985.

Dharmarakshita. *Wheel of Sharp Weapons.* Dharamsala, India: Library of Tibetan Works and Archives, 1981.

Dilgo Khyentse Rinpoche. *Enlightened Courage.* Ithaca, N.Y.: Snow Lion Publications, 2006.

Dondrub, Thubten. *Spiritual Friends.* Boston: Wisdom Publications, 2001.

First Dalai Lama. *Training the Mind in the Great Way.* Translated by Glenn H. Mullin. Ithaca, N.Y.: Snow Lion Publications, 1993.

Gampopa. *The Jewel Ornament of Liberation.* Translated by Khenpo Konchog Gyaltsen. Ithaca, N.Y.: Snow Lion Publications, 1998.

Gyaltsen, Geshe Tsultrim. *Mirror of Wisdom.* Long Beach, Calif.: Thubten Dhargye Ling, 2000.

Gyatso, Lobsang. *The Harmony of Emptiness and Dependent-Arising.* Dharamsala, India: Library of Tibetan Works and Archives, 1992.

H. H. Tenzin Gyatso, the Fourteenth Dalai Lama. *The Buddhism of Tibet.* Ithaca, N.Y.: Snow Lion Publications, 2002.

H. H. Tenzin Gyatso, the Fourteenth Dalai Lama. *Cultivating a Daily Meditation.* Dharamsala, India: Library of Tibetan Works and Archives, 1991.

H. H. Tenzin Gyatso, the Fourteenth Dalai Lama. *The Dalai Lama at Harvard.* Ithaca, N.Y.: Snow Lion Publications, 1989.

H. H. Tenzin Gyatso, the Fourteenth Dalai Lama. *Kindness, Clarity, and Insight.* Rev. ed. Ithaca, N.Y.: Snow Lion Publications, 2006.

H. H. Tenzin Gyatso, the Fourteenth Dalai Lama. *Healing Anger.* Ithaca, N.Y.: Snow Lion Publications, 1997.

H. H. Tenzin Gyatso, the Fourteenth Dalai Lama. *Path to Bliss.* Ithaca, N.Y.: Snow Lion Publications, 1991.

H. H. Tenzin Gyatso, the Fourteenth Dalai Lama. *Path to Enlightenment.* Ithaca, N.Y.: Snow Lion Publications, 1995.

H. H. Tenzin Gyatso, the Fourteenth Dalai Lama. *The Way to Freedom.* San Francisco: Harper, 1994.

Gyatso, Thubten. *Transforming Problems.* Singapore: Amitabha Buddhist Centre, 1999.

Jinpa, Thupten, trans. *Mind Training: The Great Collection.* Boston: Wisdom Publications, 2006.

Khandro Rinpoche. *This Precious Life.* Boston: Shambhala, 2003.

Lhundrub, Ngorchen Konchog. *The Three Visions.* Ithaca, N.Y.: Snow Lion Publications, 2002.

Loden, Geshe Acharya Thubten. *Path to Enlightenment in Tibetan Buddhism.* Melbourne, Australia: Tushita Publications, 1993.

McDonald, Kathleen. *How to Meditate*. Rev. ed. Boston: Wisdom Publications, 2005.

Pabongka Rinpoche. *Liberation in Our Hands: Part One, The Preliminaries*. Howell, N.J.: Mahayana Sutra and Tantra Press, 1990.

Pabongka Rinpoche. *Liberation in Our Hands: Part Two, The Fundamentals*. Howell, N.J.: Mahayana Sutra and Tantra Press, 1994.

Pabongka Rinpoche. *Liberation in Our Hands: Part Three, The Ultimate Goals*. Howell, N.J.: Mahayana Sutra and Tantra Press, 2001.

Pabongka Rinpoche. *Liberation in the Palm of Your Hand*. Rev. ed. Translated by Michael Richards. Boston: Wisdom Publications, 2006.

Patrul Rinpoche. *The Words of My Perfect Teacher*. Translated by the Padmakara Translation Group. Boston: Shambhala, 1998.

Rabten, Geshe. *The Essential Nectar*. Boston: Wisdom Publications, 1992.

Rabten, Geshe, and Geshe Ngawang Dhargyey. *Advice from a Spiritual Friend*. Boston: Wisdom Publications, 1986.

Rinchen, Geshe Sonam. *Atisha's Lamp for the Path to Enlightenment*. Ithaca, N.Y.: Snow Lion Publications, 1997.

Rinchen, Geshe Sonam. *The Six Perfections*. Ithaca, N.Y.: Snow Lion Publications, 1998.

Rinchen, Geshe Sonam. *The Thirty-seven Practices of Bodhisattvas*. Ithaca, N.Y.: Snow Lion Publications, 1997.

Sopa, Geshe Lhundub. *Peacock in the Poison Grove*. Boston: Wisdom Publications, 2001.

Sopa, Geshe Lhundub. *Steps on the Path to Enlightenment*. 5 volumes. Boston: Wisdom Publications, 2004-.

Tegchok, Geshe Jampa. *The Kindness of Others*. Weston, Mass.: Lama Yeshe Wisdom Archives, 2006.

Tegchok, Geshe Jampa. *Transforming Adversity into Joy and Courage: An Explanation of The Thirty-seven Practices of Bodhisattvas*. Ithaca, N.Y.: Snow Lion Publications, 2005.

The Third Dalai Lama. *Essence of Refined Gold*. Translated by Glenn H. Mullin. Ithaca, N.Y.: Snow Lion Publications, 1982.

Thubten Zopa Rinpoche, Lama. *The Door to Satisfaction*. Boston: Wisdom Publications, 1994.

Thubten Zopa Rinpoche, Lama. *Transforming Problems: Utilizing Happiness and Suffering in the Spiritual Path.* Boston: Wisdom Publications, 1987.

Tsong-kha-pa. *The Great Treatise on the Stages of the Path to Enlightenment.* 3 volumes. Ithaca, N.Y.: Snow Lion Publications, 2000-2004.

Tsongkhapa, Je. *The Three Principal Aspects of the Path.* Howell, N.J.: Mahayana Sutra and Tantra Press, 1988.

Tsulga, Geshe. *How to Practice the Buddhadharma.* Boston: Wisdom Publications, 2002.

Wallace, B. Alan. *Balancing the Mind.* Ithaca, N.Y.: Snow Lion Publications, 2005.

Wangchen, Geshe. *Awakening the Mind of Enlightenment.* Boston: Wisdom Publications, 1988.

Yangsi Rinpoche. *Practicing the Path.* Boston: Wisdom Publications, 2003.

Also see:

www.thubtenchdron.org

www.sravastiabbey.org